BETWEEN *Two* GARDENS

FROM EDEN TO GETHSEMANE

BOOKS BY JANE RUBIETTA

Between Two Gardens
Quiet Places
Still Waters

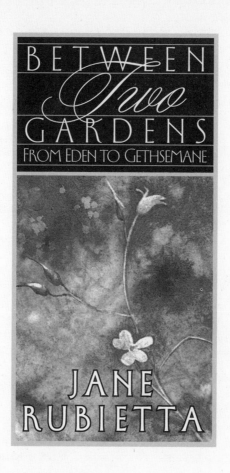

BETWEEN *Two* GARDENS

FROM EDEN TO GETHSEMANE

JANE RUBIETTA

BETHANYHOUSE

MINNEAPOLIS, MINNESOTA 55438

Published by Bethany House Publishers
A Ministry of Bethany Fellowship International
11400 Hampshire Avenue South
Bloomington, Minnesota 55438
www.bethanyhouse.com

Printed in the United States of America by
Bethany Press International, Bloomington, Minnesota 55438

Library of Congress Cataloging-in-Publication Data

Rubietta, Jane.
    Between two gardens : from Eden to Gethsemane / by Jane Rubietta.
        p. cm.
    ISBN 0-7642-2471-9 (pbk.)
    1. Gardeners—Prayer-books and devotions—English. 2. Gardens—Religious aspects—Christianity—Meditations. I. Title.
BV4596.G36 .R83   2001
242—dc21   00-012099

Between Two Gardens is dedicated
to two women whose lives and prayers
introduced me to the Gardener.
They live with Him now, and I can only imagine
their expressions of rapt joy to be with their Savior.
"Cookie" (Mary Ruth) Parker,
and my great aunt, Mae Tucker:
your love for God and for blooming things
made the world—and my heart—
a more beautiful place.

JANE RUBIETTA has a degree in marketing and management from Indiana University and has worked toward her Master's at Trinity Divinity School.

Jane's passion for soul restoration began at the bottom of a downward spiral into depression. "I lost myself trying to fulfill everyone's expectations of me. I lost sight of who God wanted me to become." She began to realize that her spiritual self-care was her own responsibility.

Jane's articles about sane soul care and restoration have appeared in nearly 100 periodicals, including *Today's Christian Woman, Virtue, Marriage Partnership, Decision, Christian Reader,* and *Christianity Today.* Prior books with Bethany House Publishers include *Quiet Places: A Woman's Guide to Personal Retreat* (1997) and *Still Waters: Finding the Place Where God Restores Your Soul* (1999). She is a dynamic speaker at conferences and retreats around the continent. Jane's husband, Rich, is a pastor, music producer, and free-lance worship leader. They have three children, and make their home surrounded by many garden opportunities in Grayslake, Illinois.

For more information about inviting Jane Rubietta to speak at a conference, retreat, or banquet, please contact her at:

Jane Rubietta
225 Bluff Avenue
Grayslake, IL 60030

Jrubietta@abounding.org

ACKNOWLEDGMENTS

"Thank you" does not begin to express the role these people have played in my life and spiritual development. Even so, inadequate as it is, a heart-felt thank-you to these special people:

To my Garden Friends in Joliet, Illinois, who tutored me in gardening: Len Hooper, Debbie Huckstep, Jackie Garton, and Kathy Fairbairn. Before that, Gayle Huebner and her magical touch with flowers impacted me profoundly.

To dear friends Kay Frahm and Ellen Binder, who, trowels and all, loaded precious keepsakes and plants and blooming bulbs into the car and trekked through horrific snow to help me create our first meditative garden at a women's retreat. From that retreat came the essence of this book. I thank God for you both!

Once again to Sandra Fricke, whose love of gardens was reflected in her careful tending of the yard that would one day become a setting in which to write *Between Two Gardens*. I'm making progress on the weeds, Sandra!

To my grandparents, who have long since gone to the ultimate Garden of Life: Bill and Betty Houpt, and Jack and Jeppie Henderson, whose luxurious plantings, whether tomatoes or roses or cotton or crocuses, form my earliest memories. Thank you for your passion for beauty.

Other special friends have kept me sowing and reaping: Shirley Mitchell (Fabulous after Fifty) and Lin Johnson (Word-Pro Communications and The Write-To-Publish Conference): they don't come better than you. Holly Griess, Lisa Lee, and Beth Elliott: your undergirding of prayer and loving laughter hold me up.

My Covenant Group, who continue to model Christlike living to me: Adele Calhoun, Karen Mains, Linda Richardson, Marilyn Stewart, and Sibyl Towner.

My ever-present Writers' Group, Lynn Austin, Joy Bocanegra, Cleo Lampos: what would I do without you?

Without Grayslake Library's excellent reference team, I would be lost in the stacks. Thank you to Carolyn Dolter, Jan Davis, Kris Buckley, Teresa Witt, Marie Hatcher, Sandy Lincoln, Kim Monaghan, Jennifer Owens, Janet Schawel. And to Mary Fitch, who coordinated my endless Interlibrary loans.

My editor for all three Bethany House books, Steve Laube, for your encouragement, persistence, and availability to listen and refine ideas with me. Thanks for picking me out of a pile of manuscripts.

To others on Team Bethany House: Jeff Braun, Alison Curtis, Melissa Smith, Judi Hedden, and Jeanne Mikkelson: you are the best. Thanks for all your patience mucking through manuscripts and creating and marketing top-notch, faith-building work. Thank you to Gary and Carol Johnson for believing in the concepts of this book.

I could not write a word without the loving support and noise level and humor of my family. Thank you for tolerating poor meals, empty refrigerators, and forgetfulness. Your growth challenges me to live out of the fullness of Christ's work in Gethsemane. Thank you, Rich, Zak, Ruthie, and Josh. I love you.

CONTENTS

INTRODUCTION

Driving through the worn neighborhood, with raw sewage running down the gutters, my heart pounded in my chest as though I'd just sprinted all the hills in the area. Could we really do what God asked of us? Had we heard that soft voice correctly? Moving from a brand new parsonage and a comfortable, supportive church in a loving, family-oriented community to this high-crime, low-income area seemed a drastic step, one requiring steady faith on the part of my pastor-husband and me. We didn't know how we would fare; only that a comfortable faith did not seem like faith, and so we had packed our home and memories and raced the moving van to this semi-urban setting. Tears rained down my face as I said good-bye to people who had nurtured my gifts and listened to my longings and urged me closer to God.

Not long into our family venture in faith, the long-neglected yards nagged at me. A hunger for another world ate at my soul, and I tore into the ugly hedges that were more weeds and poison ivy than shrubs. Rubble and rocks reminded me of all that was not fruit in my own life, and I dug and tugged. Mere arm wrestling was not enough, so I borrowed a pickax and hacked out the roots. After many blisters and bouts with poison ivy, a bit of beauty transformed my outlook and framed the entrance to our home.

Elsewhere on the same block, hidden behind a gracious two-story home in the decrepit neighborhood, a near-Eden flourished. Len had transformed his backyard into a fairyland of twinkling lights, high hedges, blooming flowers, and a fishpond that rivaled any I'd ever seen. Our toddler son was fascinated with Len's fish, and the frog that hopped about the habitat, and the lilies that bloomed at the oddest times. Once we visited in the middle of the night with a flashlight to inspect the night lily. Len became my horticultural consultant, and he shared his flowers with me when dividing time came. He told me which intriguing little sprouts would grow into garden-consuming weeds and which would one day form bouquets. Other friends, new friends from the area, bloomed in my life, and their gardening expertise also enriched my soul and brightened my world.

Soon a team of parishioners tackled the churchyard, landscaping, donating trees and shrubs, weeding, pruning, and planting. A dead tree seemed to have life within, and just as men from the church climbed around it to cut it down, they envisioned the figure of a joyful Lord, arms raised to greet His precious people. They carved away, as Michelangelo said, everything that wasn't Jesus, and dedicated the new grounds and wood carving on Easter Sunday.

Four years later, when we moved from the neighborhood I'd finally learned to call home, several perennial gardens that bloomed from early spring to late fall bolstered not only the neighborhood but also my soul. I knew when planting them that they would remain for the next pastoral family, and I prayed that the vibrant plants would be a bright spot of color in a wilted and rock-strewn world.

Hunger for Eden

Gardens continue to fascinate me with their ability to bring life and beauty to lackluster lives. In every home we've lived in since that time, I have tried to create places where God could witness to the world of His incredible creativity and love for all of us through beauty.

How much of this hunger for beauty is rooted in our exile from Eden, our longing for an idyllic place of existence? Every generation, it seems, seeks for Eden in some form or another. Various searches for paradise, for utopia, for the ideal society, for the fountain of youth and the Holy Grail have occupied and obsessed people through the ages.

Daily, catalogs and fliers filled with gorgeous flowers and promising award-winning gardens land in my mailbox. Cars jam the parking lots as people stream into stores to find the perfect seed, plant, trowel, and growth-producing compound. Weekend gardeners sweat over the curse of Adam (weeds) and mow down the grass that's sprouted up from their fertilizing efforts. Birdbaths and rock gardens and fishponds guarantee retailers a great bottom line and tempt buyers with a piece of the peace of Eden. Resort and vacation packages lure travelers with lush garden settings and the hope of genuine and permanent restoration.

Last summer, frustration drew me more deeply into the Scriptures. Looking out over our sun-parched grass, my soul thirsted for the watering of God. Even as record-breaking heat scorched the Midwest, so did the state of my soul seem to wither. Verses such as Jeremiah 31:12 sowed desire in my heart: "Their soul shall be as a watered garden" (KJV).

Jesus' repeated use of gardening terms and themes seemed

significant. "I am the vine, you are the branches," (John 15:5); "faith as a mustard seed" (Matthew 17:20); "the sower went out to sow" (Matthew 13:3). Jesus' listeners understood agriculture, farming, and hoeing out a living. Certainly Jesus spoke the language of His culture, a culture based on the fruit of the land. But, just as surely, His language points out to us a deeper importance. Because the exile that began in the Garden of Eden ends in another garden, the Garden of Gethsemane.

Parallel Gardens

Parallels exist between Eden and Gethsemane, challenging us to make the journey, to traverse the distance, beckoning us into a new, full, blooming place. In between these gardens, we find another plot of land, a place where I believe God intended to conclude the exile when He led the Israelites to the Promised Land. At the very least, Israel is a type of Eden, a place where the Lord himself would tend and toil the land:

> For the land, into which you are entering to possess it, is not like the land of Egypt from which you came, where you used to sow your seed and water it with your foot like a vegetable garden. But the land into which you are about to cross to possess it, a land of hills and valleys, drinks water from the rain of heaven, a land for which the Lord your God cares; the eyes of the Lord your God are always on it, from the beginning even to the end of the year. (Deuteronomy 11:10–12)

But this was not to be. The Israelites' refusal to enter this next garden, this place of promise, leads us into the life of Jesus, nudging us nearer to that final garden.

As we edge closer to the Garden of Gethsemane, we find Jesus returning there again and again. The Scriptures tell us that "He came out and proceeded as was His custom to the Mount of Olives; and the disciples also followed Him" (Luke 22:39). As was His custom? Yes, Jesus frequented this place, this garden. Luke 21:37 tells us that He taught during the day in the temple and at evening headed out to spend the night on the mount that is called Olive. Jesus met with His disciples in a garden, prayed in a garden, was arrested violently in a garden, and was buried in a garden tomb.

In the Garden He would wrestle once again with the Serpent of temptation; He would rely once again on the power of God to sustain Him. In the Garden, he would pray so mightily and agonize so deeply that an angel would appear from heaven, strengthening Him (Luke 22:43).

Uncomfortably, we land somewhere between two gardens, Eden and Gethsemane. Though Christ completed His work in the Garden of Gethsemane, we do not always stand in that completion. We strive for the final garden but are often mired in the mud and matted with the dust left over from Eden's exile. While we still experience some of the curses of fleeing, while we seek continually the fruit of the Promised Land, we remain, somehow, outside the gates of Gethsemane's garden.

No, we do not live in the full completion of Christ's work in Gethsemane. Suffering exists in this world; thorns continue to prick; the shame that began when Adam's and Eve's eyes were opened still paralyzes. Fear of intimacy roots us to the ground, keeping us from bonding to others and to God. We don't always hear the voice that Adam and Eve heard in the cool of the Garden; nor do we recognize Christ's voice speaking to us, and so it goes. Our fellowship is hindered, we cannot see God face to face, pain continues, and the

Serpent still tempts and throws dice for our soul.

And yet, Christ could say, "It is finished."

The parallels between and principles of the two gardens are too clear to ignore, and in the following pages I want to invite you into the fullness of all that Jesus accomplished in the Garden to end all gardens. Ultimately, the Garden of Eden finds its fulfillment in the Garden of Gethsemane—and so, I pray, shall we.

How to Use This Book

Between Two Gardens is comprised of forty readings that are appropriate at any time of the year. Using *Between Two Gardens* as a preparation for the triumph of Easter, however, will be meaningful for the individual reader and groups as well. *Between Two Gardens* will also work devotionally for those observing the calendar of the church year. Because faith must be much more than a mental exercise, each reading will have three sections after the narrative: *Listen, Learn,* and *Live.*

⊠ *Listen*

The people of Berea, in the apostle Paul's time, "received the word with great eagerness, examining the Scriptures daily, to see whether these things were so" (Acts 17:11). Any author's work is incomplete until compared with God's Word. When we listen to the Lord speak through the Scriptures, we are comparing our subject to the ultimate authority. During the listening time of each reading, we invite our gracious God to renew our minds through His Word; to speak to us anew; to prick our hearts and warm our souls.

One means of listening to Scripture with new ears is what I call "circular reading." The Latin term for this is *Lectio Divina*, or sacred reading. The process is simple: Read the passage aloud, slowly; hold the Words within your heart for a few seconds, much like savoring a rich bite of chocolate or the flavor of a charbroiled steak; and wait for God to press upon your conscious mind. Is there a phrase, a word, a verse that especially moves? You may want to write it down in a notebook, keeping track of God's intimate whispers.

Repeat the process twice more, listening in between each reading. The whisper may change, the phrase highlighted by God's Spirit may shift; the important thing is to listen afresh to the passage. Finally, invite the Lord to show you what exactly He wants you to do with His Word this day.

88 *Learn*

In this section, we learn from the thoughts of other authors, both current and classic. Because time is limited for all of us, these are sound bites, small nuggets to deepen our thinking and our application. They may provoke questions, clarify a point from the narrative, or expand on the subject matter. While we may not agree with the entire piece from which the work is excerpted, the *Learn* section is intended to make us ask questions and search for the application, to stretch us out of our comfort zone and into places of fresh, spring-green growth.

88 *Live*

Christianity was always intended to be practical, not simply intellectual, interesting, or stimulating. The *Live* section of each reading brings the subject home. "How should we then live?" Francis Schaeffer asked, and so must we not leave until we have moved closer to Gethsemane, until the truth begins to take root in our lives. This section can be used as a tool for prayer, for reflection, for journaling, or for group discussion.

Søren Kierkegaard said, "Philosophy is perfectly right in saying that life must be understood backward. But then one forgets the other clause—that it must be lived forward." This, then, is the place where we take a closer look at how the subject at hand impacts our own lives. This is the place where a mentor, if we had one, might ask us a deeply personal application question, one that makes us squirm but forces us to grow. If our lives were gardens—and gardens in Scripture are often euphemisms for the soul—here we would look for brambles and briars, pests and parasites. Here we would deadhead, plucking off faded blooms to preserve energy for new blossoms. In *Live*, we create space for new growth. What difference does the garden make if it makes no difference in the way we live?

In Between

For the uncomfortable time being, we hover between two gardens. Longing for the perfection of Eden, pressing onward to the fulfillment of Gethsemane, we look forward to the day when we shall be like Him, for we shall finally see Him face to face. Until that time, we stand in grace and exult in hope (Romans 5:2).

One

CREATION IN THE GARDEN

My fascination with gardens began early, after discovering the unique scent of the boxwood hedges outlining my grandparents' yard in the South. The slightest rustling of the bush emitted this pungent fragrance, and now a wisp of that particular scent immediately transports me to that simpler time of childhood and wonder. Our family traditionally made the trip to the farm over spring break each year, and I remember the crocus watch or, on the years when Easter was later in the season, the jonquils pushing through the earth, then bobbing golden trumpets on long stems. Violets, watercress, lilies of the valley—these were all Tennessee childhood beginnings.

Since then, my love of gardens has found me inhaling in herb gardens behind former plantations, getting lost in hedge gardens and rolling hoops on the green in Williamsburg, wandering presidential gardens, and even stopping the car to delight in landscaping. Gardens have lured me with their beauty, taken me on aromatic trips into history, and expanded my awareness of God's amazing, endless creativity.

John Galassi, poet and editor-in-chief at Farrar, Straus & Giroux, says, "Gardening is an art. If you see a beautiful garden, it's an expression of aesthetic understanding. And it's an expression of the personality of the person who did it. It's very poetic, I think."[1]

If this is true, then the statement about me made by my own garden is pathetic: around my yard, flowers ache for the sun because they are crowded out with weeds, or planted in the wrong places, or the soil is too acidic, or too filled with clay, or too . . . something, or not enough . . . of something. I do not know, and will not find out anytime soon, because gardening is a part-time interest that's actually given no time to bring to blossom all the beauty possible. Once a year, I go on a weeding binge and yank out weeds that are six feet tall and an embarrassment to my garden-convictions, a statement about my priorities, and undoubtedly a problem for my neighbors.

If these gardens say something about their creator, then the message is not positive. "Good intentions, no follow-through." "Love of beauty, armchair gardener." Or perhaps, "slightly neurotic with fantastic dreams."

But the original garden, the Garden of Eden, has much to say about the Creator. Messages about rest, and light, and beauty. Come with me as we journey through the gardens of time.

1. REST IN THE GARDEN

Our need to be needed preys upon our need for rest, and we turn on pagers, lunge for telephones, and neurotically check our e-mail, answering machine, and voice mail. I've met people who claim they sleep with their pagers on. We drag out of bed, slam the snooze button, and crawl back to the warm covers and four more minutes of oblivion. Fatigue hammers our nervous system and fills our blood with sludge. In a world where communication has become a nightmare of technology, where instant accessibility increases our prospects of success as well as the looming nearness of insanity, the Creation account reminds us of our priorities, or at the very least, of God's.

Rest in Eden

In the order of creation, *rest*-ful night came before the working day, assuring us that rest is part of the natural rhythm and restoration of our fragmented lives. "And there was evening and there was morning, one day" (Genesis 1:5). In the Jewish calendar, the "day" begins at sundown, forcing followers to start each twenty-four-hour period with rest at the top. All else proceeds from the time of rest.

This is telling, in a world that spiritualizes exhaustion, wearing it as a merit badge. Not enough sleep, and we perch on the brink of madness, of psychosis. We carry our weariness deep in our bones and settle for second best when we work first and refuse to rest. We run on caffeine, and adrenaline, and fear.

And yet, God set up a pattern in those first days of creation. There was evening and there was morning, the second day. Evening and morning, a third day. Evening and morning, a fourth day. All the way through until the seventh day of the first week, when we read, "And by the seventh day God completed His work which He had done; and He rested on the seventh day from all His work which He had done. Then God blessed the seventh day and sanctified it, because in it He rested from all His work which God had created and made" (Genesis 2:2–3).

Rest-less Between the Gardens

The Scriptures are not clear as to whether Adam and Eve waited for another week to roll around to test out the whole "day of rest" theory. Perhaps they would not have succumbed to temptation if they had observed a day of rest in between, a day to remember their priorities and their Creator, and to trust. All we know is that ever since the expulsion from the Garden, human beings have been on a fast track. Murder and mayhem fill the very next chapter of the book and lead us to Noah.

Amazingly, his name means "rest." Lamech, his father, said, "This one shall give us rest from our work and from the toil of our hands arising from the ground which the Lord has cursed" (Genesis 5:29). Whether Noah would provide rest from farming because it's difficult to farm in a flood or because his life would be one of trust and obedience, I leave to you to decide. We do know, however, that Noah learned something about the meaning of his name and tried to live into it. Genesis 6:9 reads, "Noah was a righteous man, blameless in his time; Noah walked with God."

But the rest was short-lived. The very next generation filled its lives with shame, and the cycle of trust and toil was again turned askew. They, too, toiled so much they could not trust, until God led them to the Promised Land. "I begged you to enter my rest, but you would not." Thankfully, God has not left us *rest-less*. As Warren Wiersbe wrote, "Noah means 'rest.' Mankind was in misery and longed for the promised Redeemer to come. He *has* come, and we can come to Him and find true rest."[2]

True Rest: Through Gethsemane to the Cross

Since the evacuation from Eden, we have grasped for the brass ring, only to learn that we clutch a painted, peeling, pockmarked piece of trash. We have underrated rest and overrated its second-best companion, work. What cataclysmic and colossal messes we make when we continue to live in a land without rest. Catastrophe and captivity and chaos accelerate until we come to the gentle Christ child, who urges us to put our necks with His in the yoke, that instrument of work, and find rest (Matthew 11:29).

When we move through the Garden of Gethsemane to the cross, we find that all our work is brokenness, and only the cross, only the crucified and risen Christ, brings rest. "Come to me, all who are weary and heavy-laden, and I will give you rest" (Matthew 11:28).

"And the man has begun to be strong who has begun to know that, separated from life essential, that is God, he is weakness itself, but of strength inexhaustible if he be one with his origin," wrote George MacDonald.[3] When we approach Christ, open our clenching fists, and lay down our armor of work and fatigue, we find again that oneness with Him, that irreplaceable rhythm of trust and toil.

And it was evening, and it was morning. Today.

Rest Today

The bright woman next to me at dinner talked animatedly about her faith and her decision to rest after twenty-six years of practicing law. "With the money I had earned, I chose to buy myself time. I quit my job and began to think about the direction of my life," she stated, smiling, clearly at peace with her choice. She found that listening time brought with it refreshing renewal, that rest really did restore her tattered and battle-weary soul.

Not everyone can afford to quit work and reflect on life. Others at the table had taken two weeks out of their lives, vacation time for most of them, to fill themselves with Scripture and rest in that full-ness. Rest, they were finding, clears the mind of rubble and weari-ness, sharpens the focus, purges the panic and fuzzy thinking.

Does two weeks sound like too much? What about resting from technology for a twenty-four-hour period? Decide which communi-cation tool enslaves you the most, and cut the cord of dependency for a period of time. Julia Cameron, creativity specialist, suggests that word lovers rest for an entire week from words: all media, in-cluding books, newspapers, television, radio, and computer. Rest for a week from other people's words, and see if you don't find new words within; see if you don't find the Word of God once again living and active in the deep part of your soul.

And, as an additional leap of faith, what about tucking in at night at a decent time—shutting off all lights and nestling up to the One, the only One, who grants us rest? And how about going to sleep without a rash of rationale? As the inimitable G. K. Chesterton said,

> For those who study the great art of lying in bed there is one
> emphatic caution to be added. Even for those who can do their
> work in bed (like journalists), still more for those whose work
> cannot be done in bed (as, for example, the professional har-
> pooner of whales), it is obvious that the indulgence must be very
> occasional. But that is not the caution I mean. The caution is
> this: if you do lie in bed, be sure you do it without reason or
> justification at all. . . . If a healthy man lies in bed, let him do it
> without a rag of excuse; then he will get up a healthy man. If he
> does it for some secondary hygienic reason, if he has some sci-
> entific explanation, he may get up a hypochondriac.[4]

Truly there is no need to rationalize or explain our need of rest. Rest restores, and rest reminds us of Augustine's wisdom, "Thou hast made us for Thyself, and our hearts are restless until they find their rest in Thee." May you find your rest in God. Because first there is evening, and then there is morning.

⌘ *Listen*

Then it will come about in that day that the nations will resort to the root of Jesse, who will stand as a signal for the peoples; and His resting place will be glorious.

Isaiah 11:10

There remains therefore a Sabbath rest for the people of God. For the one who has entered His rest has himself also rested from his works, as God did from His.

Hebrews 4:9–10

⌘ *Learn*

The greatest act of faith that a man can perform is the act that we perform every night. We abandon our identity, we turn our soul and body into chaos and old night. We uncreate ourselves as if at the end of the world: for all practical purposes we become dead men, in the sure and certain hope of a glorious resurrection.

G. K. Chesterton,
Lunacy and Letters

⌘ *Live*

✦ What part does rest play in your relationship with God?
✦ What keeps you from resting?

2. Light in the Garden

As a toddler, some of my son Joshua's favorite music came from "The Beginner's Bible," sung by Jodi Bensen (of *Little Mermaid* fame). The opening number sang the wonders of creation, the glories of those first days. My heart, too, always quickened when the words, "And God said, 'Let there be light!' " rang out.

Light in Eden

God created light, and split the night in two. The possibilities of light, the promise inherent in light, move me: light illuminates, opens up, eliminates darkness, establishes freedom, eradicates fear. The absence of darkness is the presence of light, and God graciously gave us light. Darkness may allow for sleep and growth and recovery—ah, but light . . . light opens up the world. And the right amount of light is crucial in gardens.

Light Between the Gardens

Last year I went on a planting frenzy and stuck hundreds of bulbs capriciously in the ground. In a yard that is easily half shade— and the parts that aren't shaded are places one walks, not plants— finding a hundred slots for those bulbs was difficult. I decided to plant one of my favorite flowers, the iris, next to the hostas, thinking the hosta leaves would hide the iris leaves as those began to decay. But hostas are shade plants, primarily, and evidently iris thrive in sun, not shadow. When I remembered to look for the blooming plants in May, I found them weakly sporting emaciated blooms, and nearly horizontal in their beds.

Light changes the world. And God used light to set in motion growth and rest and guidance. The absence of light meant it was time to trust, to rest in God's care, to allow Him to carry the world for a spell. When God's presence filled the tabernacle or temple, the glowing evidence was called the "Shekinah glory." Angels are introduced frequently in the Scriptures with light, with "radiant beams." Lest we forget the Serpent's ousting from Eden, we must remember that Satan masquerades as "an angel of light" (2 Corinthians 11:14). God used light, in the form of a towering pillar of fire, to lead the way across the wilderness to the Promised Land.

The Light of the World

God continues to lead us with light, to show us the path, to guide us into truth. When we come to the New Testament, the book of John opens up with, "In him was life, and that life was the light of men. The light shines in the darkness, but the darkness has not understood it. . . . The true light that gives light to every man was coming into the world" (1:4–5, 9 NIV). The vital nature of this light becomes even more clear when we consider the total eclipse of light on Calvary when Christ was crucified. Darkness fell upon the earth for three hours.

That this light gives light to all is seen by a parallel analogy in our world today. The invention of the electric light by Thomas Edison in the 1800s changed the world. Not only did he give the gas companies (which controlled the only form of light except for candles and oil) a run for their money, he also ran the wires for a whole new world. Almost all of our technology today springs from those experiments and failures and ultimately the invention of the light bulb.

And our entire spiritual lives hang on Christ, who said of himself, "I am the light of the world; he who follows Me shall not walk in the darkness, but shall have the light of life" (John 8:12). Jesus is compared to the rising sun (Luke 1:78–79) and the morning star (2 Peter 1:19), and in heaven, we'll have no need of the sun by day or the moon by night, "for the glory of God has illumined it, and its lamp is the Lamb. And the nations shall walk by its light, and the kings of the earth shall bring their glory into it" (Revelation 21:23–24).

Light Essential, Light Now

Without light, life is in danger. Light is being studied for treatment for chronic pain, autism, depression, and cancer, among other illnesses.[5] Only a few minutes of sunlight each day triggers production of bone-strengthening vitamin D, and sunlight is crucial in combating rickets. High rates of depression, alcoholism, and suicide in Alaska, where there are mere minutes of light in winter months, reinforce the importance of light.

Just as we can't live without light, we can't know true light without the light of Christ. In the Jewish culture, light represented God's holiness, and when the light of the glory of God shines in our hearts, when we become children of the light (John 12:36), we take up that light for others. Christ's own words make clear our position and the responsibility with the light entrusted to us:

You are the light of the world. A city set on a hill cannot be hidden. Nor do men light a lamp, and put it under the peck-measure, but on the lampstand; and it gives light to all who are in the house. Let your light shine before men in such a way that they may see your good works, and glorify your Father who is in heaven. (Matthew 5:14–16)

Christ, the Light of the World, transfers that flame to us. Too often, we hide the light, the brightness, the glory of God. Not wanting to seem boastful or proud, not wanting to stir comparison in others, we minimize God's light and action in our lives. But, even as we have life in the light, so we share the life-light with others. And our lives, which were delivered from the domain of darkness, become a welcome invitation to others to join us in the light.

The light of Christ burns away the shadows of the soul, throwing wide the windows of our lives, that others might enter in and they, too, find light and life.

No wonder God said, "Let there be light."

✠ *Listen*

. . . because of the tender mercy of our God,
by which the rising sun will come to us from heaven
to shine on those living in darkness
and in the shadow of death,
to guide our feet into the path of peace.

Zechariah's prophecy,
Luke 1:78–79 NIV

So justice is far from us, and righteousness does not reach us.

We look for light, but all is darkness; for brightness, but we walk in deep shadows.

Like the blind we grope along the wall, feeling our way like men without eyes.

At midday we stumble as if it were twilight; among the strong, we are like the dead.

Arise, shine, for your light has come, and the glory of the Lord rises upon you.

See, darkness covers the earth and thick darkness is over the peoples,

But the Lord rises upon you and his glory appears over you.

Nations will come to your light, and kings to the brightness of your dawn.

Isaiah 59:9–10, 60:1–3 NIV

🞖 *Learn*

There is at the back of all our lives an abyss of light, more blinding and unfathomable than any abyss of darkness; and it is the abyss of actuality, of existence, of the fact that things truly are, and that we ourselves are incredibly and sometimes almost incredulously real. It is the fundamental fact of being, against not being; it is unthinkable, yet we cannot unthink it, though we may sometimes be unthinking about it; unthinking and especially unthanking. For he who has realized this reality knows that it does far outweigh, literally to infinity, all lesser regrets or arguments for negation, and that under all our grumblings there is a subconscious substance of gratitude. That light is the positive business of the poets, because they see all things in the light of it more than do other men.

G. K. Chesterton,
Chaucer[6]

88 *Live*

- ✦ When do you shy away from the light? Why?
- ✦ How have you cultivated time in the light of Christ?
- ✦ In what way can you share that light today?

3. BEAUTY IN THE GARDEN

As our rental car rounded the curve and dipped into the park, my heart faltered. My first response to the Garden of the Gods, in Colorado Springs, was tremulous, gasping, teary-eyed. The breath was wrenched from my mouth as I saw the incredible sculptures erupting from the ground in their red-hued glory. No one but God could create such breath-stealing statues. After walking around in the baking sun, sweating and tromping through the clay-colored dust, though, I began to focus on my discomfort and grew numb to the glory. Isn't that a common frailty? Confronted by the majesty of God, all we can think of is the blister on our right foot.

Beauty in Eden

Adam and Eve, it seems, also grew numb to the beauty of Eden. Very quickly they reached for the only item forbidden to them. Had Eden lost its attraction? Had they become bored so quickly? As they lost their footing in the Garden soil, Adam and Eve began a life of longing—a longing for beauty that continues, unrequited, until we are once again united with God.

Longing for Beauty Between the Gardens

God has provided us with a complete picture of His loving, longing heart! He's written His love for us across the entire sky. The whole universe is a testimony glowing, vivid, vibrant, pulsing with the most amazing living love letter. Gardens—beauty—appeal to us on many levels—the longing for beauty, for emotional connection, for life and love and future. More than anything, the endless beauty of God's creation cries out against our crowded lives, begging us to listen to those longings.

Beauty brings us into places of healing, as well as into God's presence. In *Gesundheit!* the book written by Patch Adams and Maureen Mylander and brought to light by the Robin Williams movie *Patch Adams*, a patient and Patch are outside. The patient suffers from a form of arthritis that destroys the spine and all major joints in the body. The patient tells the story, "We watched a beautiful orange sunset in silence, and Patch turned to me and said, 'Do you have arthritis while you're watching this?' The question floored me. 'No, come to think of it, I don't.' "[7]

Gareth, the patient, hadn't noticed the absence of pain until Patch asked him; so, I think, do we not notice when the very hills cry out the presence of God. Perhaps my own fascination with gardens has been rooted in the need to be increasingly aware of God's presence—loving, creative, forgiving. Finding, seeking out those places—whether taking time to notice the giant trees out my window or the intricate fabric of a dragonfly's wings—has forced me out of my treadmill existence and into God's grace.

Christ in the Gardens

So much of the drama in Christ's life took place in beautiful settings. The baptism in the river, teaching His disciples on the

Mount of Olives, speaking on the waterfront, all-night prayer in His favorite garden. Burial and resurrection in a garden. Christ's encounter with Mary Magdalene, and the healing of her grief, in the Garden early in the morning.

Christ understood that intimacy and healing and learning are enhanced by beauty. Because He was always centered, always in touch and attentive to the Father, His strategic settings must have been for our sakes.

> The heavens declare the glory of God; the skies proclaim the work of his hands. Day after day they pour forth speech; night after night they display knowledge. There is no speech or language where their voice is not heard. Their voice goes out into all the earth, their words to the ends of the world. (Psalm 19:1– 4 NIV)

In the words of the old hymn, "God, who touchest earth with beauty, make my heart anew; With thy spirit recreate me, pure and strong and true."[8] When God heals us of our deformity, the misshapenness of soul that comes from separation from Him, our lives become hedged with beauty, and even as the heavens declare the glory of God, so the gardens of our lives beckon others to come and find healing.

As God began it all in Eden, He grants us another beginning in Gethsemane. The painful separation from God in Eden is put back together in Gethsemane. What began at a tree ends at the gruesome tree of the cross.

🞝 *Listen*

I will heal their apostasy, I will love them freely, for My anger has turned away from them. I will be like the dew to Israel; he will blossom like the lily, and he will take root like the cedars of Lebanon. His shoots will sprout, and his beauty will be like the olive tree, and his fragrance like the cedars of Lebanon. Those who live in his shadow will again raise grain, and they will blossom like the vine.

Hosea 14:4–5

⊞ *Learn*

Have the unspoken yearnings of our soul been put there to draw us to the living God, a lover who dances into our dreams and schemes with the promise of fulfillment? Is He flirting with us when He sprays the sky with a multihued sunset or shatters the silence with frightening roars of thunderclap? Does He watch our wonder and wait to see if we're impressed as He leaps in the shadows for joy over His works? If so, what are we to do? How are we to respond to such magnificent exhibitions?

—Tricia McCary Rhodes,
Taking Up Your Cross:
The Incredible Gain of the Crucified Life

⊞ *Live*

+ Where are you most aware of the presence of God?
+ What places of beauty are easily accessible to you? How often do you go there?
+ Where have you encountered beauty when none was visible?

Two

ONENESS IN THE GARDEN

I come to the garden alone
While the dew is still on the roses,
And the voice I hear
Falling on my ear,
The Son of God discloses.

And he walks with me, and he talks with me,
And he tells me I am his own;
And the joy we share as we tarry there,
None other has ever known.
  C. Austin Miles, 1913, "In the Garden"

Longing swelled within me as I heard the words to the old hymn "In the Garden." How wonderful it would be to hear God's voice, intimate and distinct, definite with instruction and rich with love. What was it like for Adam and Eve to open their eyes and see God, and hear His voice? Or for Enoch, who walked with God? Or for Moses, whose face was so bright from his time with God on the mountain that he wore a veil for fear others would be scorched or blinded? Now, our eyes are veiled, shadowed; we cannot *see* Him face to face. We cannot physically *walk* with Him, as Mary Magdalene walked that dew-filled morning when Christ met her in the Garden after Gethsemane's anguish, in the Garden of the new tomb.

Frustration often fills me: I want to hear God's voice, urgent and clear as a melody; I want marching orders, a sign to reveal exactly what to do next, where to go. I want the towering pillar of fire to lead me, an enormous cloud to camp in front of me, telling me when it's safe to move on again. But I cannot hear, cannot see; the cataracts of humanity dim my vision so that I am not always aware that God is present, ever-loving and gently taking my hand along the path of life.

And there, I guess, my humanity shows up again: that base element that insists on answers, on guidance, and forgets about relationships. Our culture as a whole wants results; I am no different, it seems. What I *want* to want is a relationship. Too often I want the benefits of that unbroken relationship without the accompanying responsibility.

After a year crammed with traveling and speaking, sometimes as often as fifteen times a month, I cried out to God. "I have no friends, no fellowship. This aloneness reveals my brokenness. I cannot go on like this, nor is this pleasing to you." I wept after leaving my children and husband, and was so exhausted upon returning that I could not enter gladly or easily or fully into their lives.

This aloneness and lack of connection didn't just alarm *me*; it alarmed my covenant group, that group of godly women who ask insightful questions about my life and my faith and God's call. Months had passed since I'd attended our monthly meeting, and as I shared my soul, their loving, thoughtful silence deepened and a holiness seemed to fill the room. And they, too, echoed the voice of

God in my innermost being, that voice ever calling, "Where are you?" It is not good, no, nor is it safe, to live in fissured fellowship. I not only failed to abide by His command to rest, I had isolated myself from those whom God had provided to me for support.

This was not the Master Gardener's plan. Adam and Eve demonstrated for us first unbroken and then broken companionship; from the time of their creation in Eden through their exile, we see our own patterns of longing, choice, and their consequences. En route to Gethsemane, Jesus reestablishes the possibility for unbroken fellowship in His life, death, and resurrection.

4. UNBROKEN IN EDEN

Adam and Eve model for us the first unbroken fellowship with God, reflecting God's longing for intimate and continual communication with us. Their existence in Eden was protected—like an unborn infant in a mother's womb. Adam and Eve didn't know what they had. They had it made there in the Garden, walking and talking with God. In their sinless state, they were able to look on God, something that we, as their heirs, cannot do in our fallenness. "No one can see God and live" (see Exodus 33:20).

Perhaps we all crave that connection, a craving that pulsed within Adam's and Eve's hearts from the moment God formed them and breathed life into their nostrils. For us, the longing is easily disguised and fended off by our bustling, our buying, our constant list-making and planning. This yearning still rears its head, however, in our relationship-hopping, in the perfection-seeking drive within us that abandons friends when they disappoint us, in our fleeing of intimacy when the risk of being known threatens. If we listen to our lives, if we pay attention to the patterns we live out, we will recognize this hunger for what it is: a deep soul-longing for a seamless reconnection with God.

God called, they heard. God freely walked about the Garden of Eden. Imagine knowing that God, the Creator of all the earth, was right on the other side of the hedges, or strolling down the path lined with flowering trees, wanting time with you! Imagine knowing that you might run into Him as you round a bend, hear Him whistling down the next row; imagine anticipating seeing God at any moment. Did expectancy fill Adam and Eve? Did their hearts beat in a crazy, lopsided rhythm, some combination of the heartthrob of meeting a lover, the joy of seeing a best friend, and the happy clapping of a child seeing Daddy?

This is hard to picture in a world dressed in fatigue, where we are too tired to give much notice to the visible, tangible people in our lives. In a society numbed by the severing of relationships even as our bodies grow numb when a nerve is severed, the possibility of living in unbroken connection with anyone, let alone God, is farfetched. And it might involve a great deal of work on our parts, which means spending time, a scant commodity. But it is appealing to imagine, to put ourselves in the place of Adam and Eve, to ponder the opportunity to watch for God on the path, expecting fully to see Him at the next bend.

Surely in the same setting we would heed that call; surely we would hasten to His side, place our hand in His, listen and laugh and intensely love Him.

But no. Experience shows that we, too, would choose as Eve chose, respond as Adam responded.

⊠ Listen

" 'You shall love the Lord your God with all your heart, and with all your soul, and with all your mind, and with all your strength. . . . You shall love your neighbor as yourself.' There is no other commandment greater than these."

Mark 12:30–31

For that which I am doing, I do not understand; for I am not practicing what I would like to do, but I am doing the very thing I hate.

Romans 7:15

⊠ Learn

Connection is disappearing from modern life because a part of us wants it to. We want to get rid of the discomfort of the human moment. We want speed, efficiency, and control. Then we want rest and relaxation. The best way to achieve these goals is to deal with people as little as possible. They just get in the way!

Edward M. Hallowell,
Connect

⊠ Live

✦ What keeps you from closeness in relationships? With God, with yourself, with friends? When do you recognize that craving and how do you avoid its fulfillment?

✦ In a sentence, state your deepest longing for intimacy.

✦ Are there people in your life who "just get in the way"? What is the best way to deal with them?

5. Broken in Eden

Seeing God, hearing Him walk about, they reached for something that looked like life but really contained death. For them . . . for us. Adam and Eve chose, perhaps unwittingly, perhaps not knowing fully the consequences of their choice. They chose knowledge, extending the right hand of fellowship to the fallen angel, Satan, in the form of a serpent. They preferred the power that comes with knowledge (eating from the tree of the knowledge of good and evil) to the constant companionship of their Friend and Creator.

Tempted by Satan's bait, "God knows that in the day you eat from in . . . you will be like God" (Genesis 3:5), they snatched power over unbroken fellowship. And they broke forever the possibility of seeing God face to face, until the coming of the Lord Jesus, the promised Messiah.

This is coveting in its most naked, glaring form: it was Satan's sin in heaven before he fell; it was Adam and Eve's sin; it is mine. Wouldn't being *like* God be better than to *rely on* God, especially now, when we cannot even see God? We are uncomfortable with the unseen, with the walk by faith—with mystery. Like Adam and Eve, we choose to *know*, to be like God in seizing control, shielding our vulnerabilities, withdrawing when people get too close or when intimacy requires being real.

The first couple listened to the wrong voices. Eve listened to the Serpent's wiles, and to Adam God said, "You have listened to the voice of your wife, and have eaten from the tree . . ." (Genesis 3:17).

Not to say men should never listen to their wives, simply that the primary voice we heed must be God's. God's voice, the Word, is our ultimate sieve.

Our choices are too often death choices that separate us from hearing God, walking with Him, talking with Him, knowing His presence intimately. We listen to the wrong voice, heed the Siren's call, and walk out of the life-giving garden of communion into a world of endings, of death.

En Route to Gethsemane

After Adam and Eve fled Eden, the Scriptures recount the broken relationship. The exile was necessary, "lest [Adam] stretch out his hand, and take also from the tree of life, and eat, and live forever" (Genesis 3:22). Living forever in brokenness and separation was intolerable to God; the exile from Eden meant that reestablishing oneness remained possible.

With hope we see Enoch, who walked with God, and then "he was not, for God took him" (Genesis 5:24; see also Hebrews 11:5). In a chapter (Genesis 5) constantly tolling the death knell—"and he died," "and he died," "and he died"—Enoch's closeness with God brings a bloom of possibility to our journey toward the promised garden.

Moses' life, too, bears witness to the longing heart of God as Moses leads the people out of Egypt toward the Promised Land. The Scriptures tell us, "Thus the Lord used to speak to Moses face to face, just as a man speaks to his friend" (Exodus 33:11). So holy was their relationship that Moses' face glowed from being in God's presence; he veiled the brillance of his face when returning to the Israelites. The possibility of oneness with God shines, as does the reality of brokenness when Moses begs God, "Show me Thy glory!" and God responds, "You cannot see My face, for no man can see Me and live!" (Exodus 33:18, 20). But God's longing, loving heart allowed Moses to be present when God passed by, shielding His servant from death.

We know the end of that chapter in the history of the Israelites. They refused to enter that next garden, the Promised Land, out of fear and forgetfulness. Fear often whispers through my own heart, even as it spread through the Israelites' camp like fog. I forget God's faithfulness and back away from His promise to remain in me, to hold me, to provide for me. I sever connections even as loneliness wraps around my soul.

Yet, Jesus waits. His life continually reminds us of the possibility of oneness with Him, of unbroken relationship.

88 *Listen*

Behold, the Lord's hand is not so short that it cannot save; neither is His ear so dull that it cannot hear. But your iniquities have made a separation between you and your God, and your sins have hid His face from you, so that He does not hear.

Isaiah 59:1–2

88 *Learn*

If you want to change, you can. The best way to change is through changing your connections, deepening them, expanding them, maybe eliminating a few, pruning others, and fertilizing still others. You may develop a new friendship, or deepen your connection to beauty, or develop your connection to God, or make peace with a member of your family.

There are many different ways to change through changing your connections.

Edward M. Hallowell,
Connect

✠ *Live*

+ Where do you see the yearning for connection, and examples of its brokenness and its completion, in your own life?
+ What do you choose in the place of intimacy?
+ Where do you choose *to know* rather than to trust?
+ When have you felt God asking you to believe, to trust Him in the unseen rather than the facts, which are seen?

6. UNBROKEN: JESUS WITH GOD

Jesus' fellowship with God was unbroken in both heaven and on earth. He modeled unbroken communion with God by living in human form in 100 percent dependence on God. He did not rely on His being wholly God; no, on earth He "emptied Himself" (Philippians 2:5–8) and became fully human, living as a human being like us but in total reliance on God. I love reading Christ's conversations with others in Scripture; how often He responded to the thoughts and whisperings of others though He did not hear their audible questions or condemnation. (The story in Luke 7:36–50, of the Pharisee and the woman who anointed Him with costly perfume, is a favorite example of Jesus knowing the heart of another.) Because of His constant dialogue with God, because He always listened with His heart to the Father's voice, Jesus addressed their thoughts with piercing accuracy.

Broken

Jesus depended entirely on God. This is why, in that night of darkness and heart-splitting prayer in the Garden, He could plead with God to take the cup of suffering away from Him, but then say, "not My will but Yours." Until that moment of utter abandonment on the cross—"my God, my God, why have You forsaken Me?"—Jesus' relationship with the Father was never fractured. Only when He took upon himself the weight and hideousness of our sin was God forced to hide His face from His only Son, because "no one can see God and live." To save us, to provide for us the possibility of fellowship with God, Christ had to sever His own relationship with God.

We do not know the agony God experienced in those hours of separation from His Son, nor that of His Son as He wrestled, alone, for the final time with the serpent, Satan. The Scriptures do not tell us; we can only touch the edges of that rib-squeezing grief. And here, too, we can almost feel the intensity of God's heartbreak when we are separated from Him, when the darkness of sin hides His face from us.

Unbroken

Imagine that moment when He burst forth from the clutches of death itself—how the trumpets must have blown in heaven! What rejoicing, what a celebration—the One who was dead is now living!

What heavenly hymns must have heralded Jesus' victory. He rose and was reunited immediately in His spirit with His Father and physically with His beloved friends on earth. When He returned to heaven, Jesus left behind His Spirit, that we would never again be disconnected from Him.

Never again can death separate us from God—nor can life! Because Christ bore the agony of separation for us, we need never be apart again.

⚏ Listen

For I am convinced that neither death, nor life, nor angels, nor principalities, nor things present, nor things to come, nor powers, nor height, nor depth, nor any other created thing, shall be able to separate us from the love of God, which is in Christ Jesus our Lord.

Romans 8:38–39

⚏ Learn

Communion with God—that deep-felt, unbroken bond of love—kept Jesus steady, moved Him along the path to Golgotha, sustained Him in the Garden of Gethsemane, and allowed Him to be pounded to the Cross. It was only when He took on the sins of the world that the bond of love was broken.

Jane Rubietta

⚏ Live

- ✦ When are you most separated from God?
- ✦ When have you experienced Him reaching out to you,

calling you by name, establishing a connection with you?
✦   What keeps you from an immediate response?

7. BROKEN RELATIONSHIPS

Unrealistic Expectations

Relationships, whether with God or with others, begin to break down when we overload them with unrealistic expectations. The disciples' expectations of Jesus—that He would be a reigning monarch like other political leaders; that He would deliver them immediately from physical oppression; that His power would look like the power of other kings—these expectations kept them from truly listening to what Jesus told them about himself. Ultimately, they fled at His death, denying Him and fracturing their relationship, because they expected something far different than He delivered.

Our relationships break down when we expect others to be what they are not and cannot accept them for who they truly are. As a newlywed, and later as a pastor's wife, I expected that my husband's primary role would be to meet all my needs: he should be my lover, my confidant, my best friend, my spiritual advisor, my physical trainer; he should also be good with a checkbook. Without processing our own needs and expectations in relationships, we're in danger of sinking them.

In our churches we often see the fracturing of fellowship due to unrealistic expectations. Disunity in the church may be caused by a need to feel valued and valuable, and may look like the disciples jostling for the seat at Jesus' right hand. Rather than work at staying in relationship, at the first sign of discord we may jump ship, leave the church, drop out of the life of faith because the other didn't prove to be perfect or had more gifts than we had. Unity with one another is a sign of our oneness with God. This fracturing of relationships in the church is another sign of our brokenness, our separation. Rather than giving cause for judgment of another, it demonstrates our need to live in constant communication with God.

False Impressions

Relationship fractures also occur when we give others false impressions of ourselves. In college, I pretended to exercise for the fun of it, though I can't say I ever experienced a runner's high. There is nothing remotely fun about exercise as far as I can tell. When Rich and I met and married several years later, I had never gotten past the fatigue stage of exercise, but my new husband couldn't know that. He thought he was exchanging rings with someone who loved working out, and we did lift weights together (twice), and hike and bike. In spite of good companionship, on my list of enjoyable activities, exercise falls below cleaning sewer lines. This was a blow for Rich, and he felt deceived.

False impressions may stem from not truly knowing who we are and from not experiencing ourselves as beloved by God, *as is*. I didn't mean to deceive; I just never thought about the "whys" of my actions and the impressions those actions gave. Other uglier examples of false expectations and false impressions exist, but the point is, even in minor instances, these cause relationship fractures.

Ignoring Relationships

Fractures also develop when we ignore a relationship. This may seem like an excerpt from "Relationship Tips for Idiots," but it's true: we can go for days or even weeks without really talking to one another. James and Kathryn, married twenty years, found out the hard way when they went into business together. They made great business partners; their gifts were perfectly compatible for building and running a business, but soon the business talk took over their entire homelife so that they were no longer married emotionally.

Parents learn this when suddenly faced with time alone together after years of talking only about child-rearing details. The empty nest often empties out even more when the couple realizes they no longer know one another.

Susan and Karen were the best of friends, next-door neighbors, and coffee companions until a job transfer shoved a long-distance wedge between them. The space between conversations lengthened until they corresponded only with a note at Christmas, and then, finally, even those token letters stopped. Relationships are difficult to maintain and improve without time together.

Imbalance in Give-and-Take

Then, too, an imbalance in give-and-take creates problems. If a relationship seems like a monologue to you, is it really a friendship? If, for instance, Brad does all the talking and Allen does all the listening, where is the intimacy? If Nolan always helps his buddies and their families move, or fixes their cars or plumbing, and they don't help him when he needs help, where is the balance? Always giving, never receiving—or the opposite—shows imbalance.

This is true for our relationships with one another and our relationship with God. I used to hate prayer and didn't feel particularly close to God; then I realized that most of my prayer life was me telling God what to do and whom to care for. I filed away my prayer lists and filled myself up with God's Word, and waited. Paid attention. Loved God by ceasing my jabbering, controlling, working. And, amazingly, became more aware of God's love for me. Then, carrying concerns about others to Him, I freely released the burdens into His capable care.

As we grow in our ability to recognize relationship blocks and to examine our own responsibilities in their creation, we become able to sustain those relationships. Living in constant communion with others and with God cannot be impossible, or Jesus couldn't have demonstrated that intimacy. As we listen more, we will recognize the voice of God speaking to us, in silence, in the Word, and through others, for "My sheep know my voice."

✄ Listen

My sheep hear My voice, and I know them, and they follow Me; and I give eternal life to them, and they shall never perish; and no one shall snatch them out of my hand. My Father, who has given them to Me, is greater than all; and no one is able to snatch them out of the Father's hand. I and the Father are one.

John 10:27–30

✄ Learn

Our dignity is that we are children of God, capable of communion with God, the object of the love of God—displayed to us on the Cross—and destined for eternal fellowship with God. Our true value is not what we are worth in ourselves, but what we are worth to God, and that worth is bestowed upon us by the utterly gratuitous love of God. All our lives should be ordered and conducted with this dignity in view.

William Law,
Christianity and Social Order

88 *Live*

✦ Which fracturing elements do you most often use? Why?
✦ When have you overcome some of those relationship fractures?
✦ How is the Shepherd calling, leading you toward Him?

8. LISTENING TO THE VOICE

After my covenant group so graciously spoke to me in love, I knew the truth. I had been speaking in ministry so often that I spent little time listening. It's difficult to do both at the same time, and all the speaking and its troubling companion, incessant motion, had drowned out the song in my heart. One Monday, as my seasonal speaking commitments neared their end, deep joy welled up within. Over and over the words to Keith Green's song "There Is a Redeemer" rushed up from my soul and burst out in music.

When our eight-year-old tore into the house after school, he braked in surprise. "Mom, I didn't know you could sing." This from a child to whom I sang endlessly while rocking, nursing, cuddling. I smiled, hugged him, and ruffled his poky hair, but my heart was sad.

Minutes later the song returned, and again, Josh exclaimed, his face filled with wonder, "I just didn't know you could sing."

The sadness took over then, tightening my throat with grief. Later I bowed before God. Stress and exhaustion and busyness had extinguished the song for so long that my children did not even know that sometimes music lived in me. This is dangerous evidence of that broken fellowship, living one life in public and a different life in private. Joy is one of the first losses when we stop listening, and as much as I love my profession, life had been decidedly joyless.

As I responded to God's pressure and presence with a string of "I'm-sorries" to speaking invitations, a lightness so filled me that I bounced around the house for days like a helium balloon. Writing became a nurturing time with God again, and my energy and laughter around my family grew.

God has handed me the microphone hundreds of times in the past year or two, and taken me around the country that others might hear His voice through my teaching (not singing). Now, it seems, He wants me to limit my own words in order to better listen to His voice, to better practice the unbroken fellowship for which I long. No, the speaking isn't sin; the issue is obedience to His call. Now obedience means less of my own voice, that I might come to know His voice all the better, and that my children, too, might come to know and love His voice, because they hear it as a joyful melody line through my own life. Then, when asked to express His message to larger groups, those words will ring with truth and power.

> He speaks, and the sound of His voice
> Is so sweet, the birds hush their singing,
> And the melody that He gave to me
> Within my heart is ringing.

And He walks with me, and He talks with me,
And He tells me I am His own;
And the joy we share as we tarry there,
None other has ever known.
　　C. Austin Miles, 1913, "In the Garden"

88 *Listen*

*These things I have spoken to you, that My joy may be in you, and that
your joy may be made full. . . .*

*But now I come to Thee; and these things I speak in the world, that they
may have My joy made full in themselves.*

John 15:11, 17:13

*What we have seen and heard we proclaim to you also, that you also may
have fellowship with us; and indeed our fellowship is with the Father, and
with His Son Jesus Christ. And these things we write, so that our joy
may be made complete.*

1 John 1:3–4

88 *Learn*

*I have community with others and I shall continue to have it only
through Jesus Christ. The more genuine and the deeper our community
becomes, the more will everything else between us recede, the more clearly
and purely will Jesus Christ and his work become the one and only thing
that is vital between us. We have one another only through Christ, but
through Christ we do have one another, wholly, and for all eternity.*

Dietrich Bonhoeffer,
Life Together

✂ *Live*

+ What have you been asked to relinquish?
+ Where have you struggled in your choices of intimacy versus brokenness?
+ What can you begin to do to mend a fractured relationship?

Three

DARKNESS IN THE GARDEN

Josh read aloud from the camp application, "How do you feel about the dark?" He paused, pen in hand, scrunching up his face. Then, quickly, he scrawled in the blank with fourth-grade boy handwriting, "Not afraid of it."

This was the guy who once wouldn't walk into a room without a light on. Who needed accompaniment into any and all dark places. But somehow, with the form in front of him, he was able to look ahead, into the dark, and gird up his soul and forge ahead. "Not afraid of it."

I am not so brave. I am afraid of the dark, of the darkness within me—darkness that is the very worst of me, the ugliest parts of me that I hide, with varying degrees of success, from others—and darkness outside of me. Quite often, it feels as if I have no control over either darkness.

Our church went on a mission trip to an inner-city church. We, a sheltered church in between farmland and suburb, immersed ourselves in the heart of darkness in Chicago. We hammered, sawed, cleaned, painted, laughed, sang, worshiped. And then, surrounded by thick emotional darkness, tried to sleep in the sanctuary with the "crime lights"—the floodlights that illuminated any movement out-side the church—and the sirens and the uneasy night noises.

Restless on my pew, both comfort and the oblivion of sleep evaded me, and I decided to creep downstairs to their fellowship hall to journal. I felt my way down the stairs, running my hand along the wall, and halted in the total blackness on the last step. Where was the light switch? Across the room. I plunged into the darkness and rushed for the light, flipping it on.

And screamed, and leapt into a chair. Thousands of roaches swarmed across the floor, at home in the dark, panicked by the light. With my heart pounding, I crouched on the chair and tucked my bare feet underneath me, hugging my knees. Those black bugs with their crunchy shells made me shudder. Their icky, germ-carrying, darkness-loving bodies encapsulated everything I feared.

Bad things happen in the dark. Whether looking at temptation, deceit, violence, nighttime, or night noises, darkness is a breeding ground. And our gardens are no exception.

9. Temptation in the Garden

Adam and Eve

Temptation in the first garden is well documented. The lure of that which is off limits has tempted everyone from the first couple down through the generations. It reminds me of a child in a room filled with new toys and a cash register full of money. "Play with anything. It's yours. Every single item here. Oh, but leave the cash register alone." The child looks around, and the forbidden looms larger than life, more appealing than anything else in the whole world.

Temptation. To entice to do wrong by promise of either pleasure or gain. Satan knew his target, knew their weakness. Knows ours. In a world where a two-buck lottery ticket can make us millionaires, where the promise of easy gain through gambling snares many; in a world where insider trading and the stock market's ascending numbers beckon, the temptation to do wrong is immense. In this world, this brave new world, pleasure often feels like the adrenaline-rushing temptation of risk, so taking risks—whether shoplifting's thrill or seeing whether we can entice another by look or by crook of a finger—scores big on the charts.

Adam and Eve, lured by the promise of being like God, becoming little gods, bought into the lie. And our susceptibility to illicit gain—to self-serving pleasure—has not decreased through history. Everyone is fair game—including Jesus.

Jesus

Though the wilderness could hardly be called a garden, Jesus' "ordination" ceremony consisted of forty days of temptation by Satan. The Adversary's forte is twisting the Word, taking it out of context, editing it to suit his own purposes. But Jesus, the Author, knew the Word in its entirety and withstood. Jesus came against every temptation, every word from the Serpent's mouth, battling it with the Word of God.

Still, Satan would not desist. He trailed Jesus, tempting Him at every turn. In fact, the Scriptures say that Jesus was "tempted in all things as we are, yet without sin" (Hebrews 4:15). At any point,

Jesus could have succumbed to the adulation, to the temptation to use His power in a self-serving way. But His connection with God enabled Him to stay faithful, to withstand, to resist shortcuts promising easy gain. In the Garden of Gethsemane, we find Jesus, sweating drops of blood, earnestly beseeching God, "Take this cup from me" (Luke 22:42 NIV). Jesus, tempted to circumvent his calling, battled it with prayer by connecting to the power and presence of His Abba.

The next day in court, Jesus easily could have been tempted to polish His image. For most of us, the temptation to look good is powerful, but Jesus, in Luke's crucifixion account, did not shine His reputation before Pilate or Herod. He could have. In fact, Herod was "greatly pleased" to see Jesus, because "he hoped to see him perform some miracle" (Luke 23:8 NIV). The assembly before Pilate (v. 2) told an outright lie about Jesus with their accusation, "He opposes payment of taxes to Caesar," but our Lord did not respond with a word.

And poor Peter—he'd tagged along with Christ near the riverfront, when the Lord had instructed him to go catch a fish, take out the coin he would find in its mouth, and "render unto Caesar that which is Caesar's." Peter knew the truth, and could have opposed the accusation, I suppose. Christ's tools against temptation—prayer and knowing the Word of God, which is sharper than a two-edged sword—were available to Peter and are available now to us. But disciples, then and now, are vulnerable to the Serpent of temptation.

Disciples

In the Garden of Gethsemane, when Jesus rose from pleading with the Father, "May this cup be taken from me. Yet not as I will, but as You will" (Matthew 26:39 NIV), He found His companions of three years—people with whom He had built His life, whom He had tutored daily—He found them sleeping. Not once, but three times.

Jesus was amazingly patient with the disciples in their time of tempting, especially in light of His own fervent wrestling just beyond their knapsacks. Because He fought against and won over temptation, His words carry credibility and power. Jesus knew very well that the disciples could not win over temptation without prayer. With blood no doubt staining His garments from His earnest wrestling, Jesus knew that without prayer, temptation would win the battle.

But Jesus also knew that sorrow and fatigue left them vulnerable. They were exhausted with sorrow—and fatigue and sorrow both lead us into temptation. Yet the weapon, the tried and true weapon, remains the same: finding that ultimate rest in God. In Jesus' words: "Watch and pray" (Matthew 26:41 NIV).

Our temptations seem trivial in light of the Scripture records of the dark travail of Jesus' soul in the Garden. His tolerance for the disciples' sleeping through His own trial, and His tolerance for our own struggles, is sobering in light of the meaning of the original New Testament word for temptation: it is rooted in a word meaning "to pierce." We have not yet resisted "to the point of shedding blood," and yet our every temptation pierces both our soul and Jesus. He was "pierced through for our transgressions" (Isaiah 53:5).

Jesus' words to us remain the same. In time of temptation, when we are seduced by illegitimate pleasure or ill-gotten gain or even seemingly harmless thrill-seeking or image-shining, our weapons are tried and true. When sorrow and fatigue crook bony fingers at us, urging us to indulge in sleep or escape rather than war against the enemies in the Garden, we know the truth: that prayer and the Word of God enable us to withstand any temptation. In these very tools we find Christ himself: "since He Himself was tempted in that which He has suffered, He is able to come to the aid of those who are tempted" (Hebrews 2:18). Perhaps this is the greatest miracle: that in our very place of temptation, in the darkest wrestling of our souls, Christ is present.

88 *Listen*

For we do not have a high priest who cannot sympathize with our weaknesses, but one who has been tempted in all things as we are, yet without sin. Let us therefore draw near with confidence to the throne of grace, that we may receive mercy and may find grace to help in time of need.

Hebrews 4:15–16

88 *Learn*

Temptations can be useful to us even though they seem to cause us nothing but pain. They are useful because they can make us humble, they can cleanse us, and they can teach us. All of the saints passed through times of temptation and tribulation, and they used them to make progress in the spiritual life. Those who did not deal with temptations successfully fell to the wayside. . . . Peace is not found by escaping temptations, but by being tried by them. We will have discovered peace when we have been tried and come through the trial of temptation.

Thomas à Kempis

⌘ *Live*

- ✦ When are you most susceptible to temptation? In what settings?
- ✦ What effect do fatigue and sorrow have on your ability to withstand temptation?
- ✦ How have you successfully battled temptation?

10. TREASON: DECEIT IN THE GARDEN

Treason in Eden

With galling *savoir faire*, deceit sidled into Eden. The Serpent smoothly promised Eve that she'll not die—surely not!—but rather will become like God.

"The serpent deceived me, and I ate," Eve explained. Her blame came quickly, like lines in a well-rehearsed play. Did Adam and Eve know the truth immediately? That in fact, had they remained constant, they would never have known death, but now, in spite of those treacherous words, "Surely you shall not die," they had done that very thing? That while their bodies remained alive, their spirits had died, separated instantly from the God of Life, the God who would never die?

Treason Between the Gardens

The Serpent deceived them, and they passed on a heritage of deceit. We find their offspring, Cain, protesting God's question with, "What? Am I my brother's keeper?"

As though he didn't understand the ramifications of his own self-deception, as though he didn't know the truth; this is the kind of deception to which we are vulnerable. Pretending ignorance, we claim that we are innocent. "I didn't know." "I didn't think." This sort of deception shirks responsibility and keeps us out of the Garden. The deceit of blame—blaming another, blaming a substance, blaming a circumstance—is an elaborate attempt at rationalization that avoids growth and allows weeds to consume our souls.

Not long after Cain left us his legacy, we find Isaac's son Jacob, whose name means "the supplanter," living up to—or down to—his name of deception. He tricks his brother, then his father, and steals his brother's birthright as a firstborn son. He strikes a deal for a wife, and her father tricks him, substituting his elder but homely daughter in place of the one bargained for. Seven more years of labor was all it took for Jacob to earn the rights to the wife of his choice. The legacy of deceit bleeds throughout the centuries.

Treason and Gethsemane

Judas goes down in history as the most infamous traitor. Though Judas never deceived Jesus, Judas deceived their companions because he was deceived by the lure of money and power. Kissing Jesus on the cheek, he turned and handed Him over to the guards. The reality of Judas's betrayal sunk in soon after the cold silver filled his hands. He had committed treason toward the very man who had called him "friend." The poison injected his soul, and he rushed out in despair and took his own life. Even his betrayal of the very Son of God, I believe, could not have separated Judas from God for all eternity if only he had understood the saving, forgiving grace and love of his Lord. The Man who could forgive a thief hanging at His side on a stark cross, who could forgive Peter after Peter's thrice denying knowledge of Him—this Jesus was capable of redeeming even the traitorous Judas.

And Peter. Peter has become the pet of parents of prodigals, the darling of those who raised strong-willed, impetuous children, because he ultimately received Christ's forgiveness, put himself into a position of trust and obedience, and faithfully sowed the seeds of Christianity. But Peter's problem was his own deception: about himself, his own faithfulness, his own abilities, his own dark spaces of soul. Peter did not know he had the capacity to deny Christ; he could not envision such treasonous behavior. But Christ knew, foretold it, and graciously upheld Peter: "But I have prayed for you, that your faith would not fail" (Luke 22:32).

We bear striking resemblance to Adam and Eve. Certainly we are not unlike Jacob, Judas, and Peter. For do we not commit treason, like Judas, when we hand Jesus over to the world by our own sinfulness, our actions that speak not of love but of power, envy, lust? Do we not betray Christ when we are silent in the face of another's pain; when we are passive in the face of injustice; when we fail to love, to forgive, to welcome? We exchange our relationship with the Lord of Life for the few coins of self-pity, of pouting, of revenge. These power tools do not lead us to God, they separate us from Him, even as they drill holes in our relationships with others. Like Peter, we do not know the depths of our capacity for betrayal, but Christ, who prayed His way through Gethsemane and the cross, does. And yet, does not our Lord smile, still, at us, beckon us closer, and bless us with the words, "even so do I forgive you"?

❁ *Listen*

If we say that we have no sin, we are deceiving ourselves, and the truth is not in us. If we confess our sins, He is faithful and righteous to forgive us our sins and to cleanse us from all unrighteousness.

1 John 1:8–9

❁ *Learn*

We should deal with the betrayer not as an enemy, but as a friend. At the core of the psyche of the betrayer is not an evil spirit, but failed love. Betrayers do not need forgiveness that issues from the love of another, but the restoration of a love within themselves that has gone awry. This is why it is so difficult for those who have betrayed others to be received back into fellowship through repentance and forgiveness. For betrayal tears away the flesh of fellowship and friendship, leaving only the visible skeleton of love's despair. This is too terrible to look upon, and too revealing of the fear that hides in our own love, for us to tolerate. . . .

With God's love there is no insecurity and ambivalence. God's love has no seed of betrayal, as evidenced by His faithfulness toward Israel in their disobedience. The love of Jesus has no element of betrayal, as evidenced by His faithfulness even toward those disciples who fled and the soldiers who nailed Him to the cross.

Ray S. Anderson,
The Gospel According to Judas

❁ *Live*

✦ What is the most striking experience you have had of self-deception? When have you been deceived or felt betrayed by another? How do you react to betrayal or deception?

✦ When have you deceived or betrayed another? How did you find your way back to the presence of Christ, or how did Christ find you again?

11. VIOLENCE IN THE GARDEN

Violence is like a curse word in Christian circles; the air swirls with sharp intakes of breath when discussing the possibility of violence. It is the hushed, unspoken word; we think of battered wives and their vows to silence because of shame, and we refuse to mention violence in our churches and in our homes. Yet violence need not be limited to physical roughness and resultant harm. Violence is kin to the word violate, which means to break or disregard, and violence and violation subtly destroy many in the body of Christ. This violence is rooted in the paradise of the first Garden.

Eden

Violence in Eden? Violence and paradise, even the disrupted paradise we see in the Scriptures, do not coincide. And yet in Eden we find a different kind of violence, a violence that murders the spirit, a violence of soul that defaces the image of God in another. In Eden, not only did Adam and Eve violate their relationship with one another, they brought violence into the Garden when they broke God's plan for them. Their disregard for their loving Creator's provisions brutally ushered in a cycle that eclipsed the image of God in the following generations. They violated their oneness with

God in an action that resulted in instant spiritual death—self-murder—and the ramifications spread like sound waves into our own lives.

Between Two Gardens

Violence easily hides its brutal face. Some farmers used to have "fills" on their property, into which they dumped glass, tin cans, and other unburnable items, and then covered over the trash with soil. These fills weren't visible, but underneath the cover of dirt and grass, the pieces of glass and rubble would gradually work their way to the surface, one day cutting a bare foot or an animal's paw.

Anita's life was like the hidden fill. Not one single person in her church knew that during her childhood she daily witnessed violence between her parents. By the time she married, this timid woman had either heard through closed doors or personally watched, terrified on the sidelines, thousands of instances of physical, emotional, and spiritual violence. No one knew her secret until the trauma worked its way to the surface of her life, her marriage, and her family.

But aside from the "cowering under the table" sort of violence, not so obvious violence includes violation of another's soul, the breaking of spirit and of will; this, too, is violence. The force that effaces a child's natural curiosity and creativity and spontaneity—this is violence. In *The Joy Luck Club*, Amy Tan speaks of this violation:

> For all these years I kept my mouth closed so selfish desires would not fall out. . . . All these years I kept my true nature hidden, running along like a small shadow so nobody could catch me. . . . I did not lose myself all at once. I rubbed out my face over the years washing away my pain, the same way carvings on

stone are worn down by water. . . . I also remember what I
asked . . . so long ago. I wished to be found.[1]

I have encountered in myself a violence that could wound, even
kill—a violence that, unleashed, would destroy. This darkness lurks
in all of us, from the death-row prisoner to the circumspect
businessperson to the carefree child.

And what of the violence of word or of deed that maims? We
destroy the image of God when we mock, or belittle, or hold up to
ridicule or scorn. Name-calling is violence. When someone referred
to me, in my husband's presence, as "the wife," I felt violated, re-
duced to a role and minimized. What about God? When we refer
to God as "the Man Upstairs" or "the Boss" do we violate, betray,
undermine God's personal involvement in our lives?

The churning of violence continues, like a Rototiller in soft
earth, leading us to the violence in Gethsemane.

Gethsemane

Beginning with the kiss of betrayal, violence robs the Garden of
peace, as Jesus' painful prayer comes to fruition. A "multitude" invaded the quiet place, a crowd of "chief priests and officers of the
temple and elders." They emanated violence, evidently, because the
disciples immediately perceived what would happen, and eagerly
asked, "Lord, shall we strike with the sword?" And Peter, our impetuous Peter, sliced off the ear of the high priest's slave.

Jesus' response was acute: "Stop! No more of this!" He would
not counteract violence with violence, and touched the man's ear
and healed him. Violence, it seems, undermines God's purposes.
Jesus delivered a pointed question to the armed crowd: "Have you

come out with swords and clubs as against a robber? While I was with you daily in the temple, you did not lay hands on Me" (Luke 22:51–53). That the violence came from the hands of the religious establishment, the official rule watchers, shouldn't surprise us. Any time we separate ourselves from a steady relationship with God we are vulnerable to darkness.

The brutality Jesus endured while in custody turns my stomach. When I watched the movie *Jesus* (put out by Campus Crusade for Christ) I doubled over and hid my face from the horror portrayed on the screen. I want to skim over Luke's account of the beating, the spitting, the mocking, but cannot. For violence is intimately woven into each of us, and we, in the same place, would choose the same ugly, dehumanizing acts. Alexander Whyte said, "You will understand that spitting scene that night when God lets you see your own heart."[2]

Jesus' crucifixion was the ultimate act of violence: against humanity, perfection, the voice of God. And Jesus' response, the words of our gracious and redeeming Lord, break my heart and convict me. Even as they hammered spikes into His flesh and hoisted his battered, bleeding body into the air, Jesus pleaded with His Father: "Father, forgive them; for they do not know what they are doing" (Luke 23:34). Violence shredded his back, blood dripped from His wounds, bruises and welts throbbed. But Jesus, our Jesus, said, "Forgive them. They do not know what they are doing."

Perhaps my heart breaks because I, too, have shredded flesh with words; I have hammered spikes with vengeful thoughts; I have drawn blood with a glare. But the voice of the Christ returns, over and over. "Forgive them." "Forgive them." "Forgive them."

Even violence finds redemption on a barren hill called Golgotha.

⌘ *Listen*

He was oppressed and He was afflicted, yet He did not open His mouth; like a lamb that is led to slaughter, and like a sheep that is silent before its shearers, so He did not open His mouth.

Isaiah 53:7

⌘ *Learn*

O precious Redeemer... what can I say to you—you who have been spit upon and ridiculed. You whose face is now misshapen by the blows of sinners. You who bleed, and fall ... and yet utter not a word. I cry, but my tears seem a trivial testament to the torment you endure. What can I say? Nothing. Silent sorrow is my only recourse. I pray your heart can sense my grief.

Tricia McCary Rhodes,
Contemplating the Cross

⌘ *Live*

+ When have you encountered violence (or its potential) within yourself? Others? Consider not only physical violence, but emotional and spiritual violence as well.

+ How have you responded? How has God responded?

12. NIGHT IN THE GARDEN

As a child, the television show *Dark Shadows* did very little to ease my fear of nighttime. Rather, it heightened my awareness of the encroaching dark. Every siren shattering the night meant a burglar skulked outside my window, and the police were searching for the prowler. Each creaking sound shot ominous warnings through my system. The moon hanging in the sky befriended me, and I learned to love turning on a light and reading, even studying, in the middle of the dark night. Mornings I greeted with joy because night, then, had ended.

In the beginning of time God, too, separated the night from the day, making each period finite. "And the earth was formless and void, and darkness was over the surface of the deep; and the Spirit of God was moving over the surface of the waters." God created light, approved it, and then "God separated the light from the darkness. And God called the light day, and the darkness He called night" (Genesis 1:2–5). The act of naming has a sense of mastery to it. When Adam was given the privilege of naming all the animals, it was a sign of his dominion. So, when we hear God giving the darkness a name, night, we know that He has exercised His authority over the night.

This is comforting news to the small children who still crouch within us, riddled with fear at the things that go bump in the night.

Eden

Not only did day and night, light and dark exist in Eden; night also stooped at the gate, awaiting admittance to the hearts of God's beloved. When they threw open the door for doubt and greed in the form of the Serpent, Adam and Eve opened themselves up to the night, casting out the light of God from within. From then until the New Testament, we can trace the night.

Between Two Gardens

Night takes many forms. It can mean the absence of moral values, a period of darkness emotionally or spiritually, or a period of dreary inactivity or affliction. Sounds like the Israelites' journey as they drag through the pages of history. Idolatry, war, wandering, loss of faith: all these speak of night. The moral decay of the society, which frequently resulted in captivity and imprisonment for the people of God, crowds out the light and throws us into night. Depression and anger, the darker emotions: these, too, suggest the night.

Gethsemane and the End of Night

And yet, even as morning faithfully brought the ending of night to my childhood, so the coming of the Son of Man brought the ending of night to the darkness of our lives. The wise men saw His star in the east and came to worship; the shepherds saw the star, brilliant and breaking up the night, and bowed to worship. When I first heard Christ called "the morning star" (2 Peter 1:19) my breath stopped. What a glorious name for the one who ends the night!

But before ending the night, Christ endured the darkness. Nighttime found Him wrestling alone, in the Garden, with His calling. Nighttime found Him awakening His sleeping disciples, then being abandoned. Darkness brought the religious establishment with their weapons of war to arrest Him. A long night of battering in captivity preceded His journeying through the streets amid jeers and further bloodying in the midst of emotional and spiritual night. Jesus' words to the religious at His arrest deliver the haunting truth: "This is your hour—when darkness reigns" (Luke 22:53 NIV).

Darkness also symbolizes grief, and the three hours of darkness that hung over the earth while Jesus hung from the cross show the grief of heaven. The entire earth wore a mantle of mourning with its King pinioned to a tree. For the next two days, darkness and night ruled; but when Christ, the Morning Star, rose from the dead, He abolished forever the curse of darkness. Grief may endure for the night, but joy comes in the morning.

88 *Listen*

Who is among you that fears the Lord, that obeys the voice of His servant, that walks in darkness and has no light? Let him trust in the name of the Lord and rely on his God.

Isaiah 50:10

88 *Learn*

And though this world with devils filled
Should threaten to undo us,
We will not fear for God hath willed
His truth to triumph through us.
The Prince of Darkness grim
We tremble not for him;

His rage we can endure,
For lo his doom is sure;
One little word shall fell him.

Martin Luther,
"A Mighty Fortress Is Our God"

So I go on, not knowing,
I would not, if I might
I would rather walk in the dark with God
Than go alone in the light.
I would rather walk with Him by Faith
Than walk alone by sight.

Mary Gardner Brainard,
as quoted in *The Unchained Soul,*
by Calvin Miller

🞉 *Live*

✦ What effect does darkness have on you? When do you succumb to the night?

✦ How do you stand against the dark?

✦ When do you find joy in the morning?

13. GROANS IN THE GARDEN

The temptation and treason, the violence and night in the Garden, result from the bondage of a world traumatized by Eden's events. The earth, cursed because of unfaithfulness, groans in slavery. Earthquakes and sinkholes and shifting plates; drought and resultant famine; floods and tornadoes and tidal waves and El Niño and La Niña—creation groans as it waits for redemption.

The earth still bears the consequence of our sins. "How long is the land to mourn and the vegetation of the countryside to wither?" Jeremiah asks (12:4). "For the wickedness of those who dwell in it, animals and birds have been snatched away, because men have said, 'He will not see our latter ending.'"

The eighth chapter of Romans picks up this theme, as Paul describes "the anxious longing of the creation" (v. 19). The world "stands on tiptoe" (Phillips' translation), eagerly awaiting the new heaven and the new earth. Like a restless crowd anxious to view the finished masterpiece, creation groans for the unveiling of the children of God.

"And not only this," Paul says (8:23), "but also we ourselves, having the first fruits of the Spirit, even we ourselves groan within ourselves, waiting eagerly for our adoption as sons, the redemption of our body." Our bodies groan, waiting for full deliverance, as a pregnant woman waits to give birth. We wait, knowing God has good in store for us. These groanings anticipate what God will do in us, through us, with us, as He conforms us fully into the image of His Son.

Our bodies groan, too, because though our spirits are alive in Christ, our bodies are dying! (Romans 8:10) Our bodies were compromised in the first Garden, and though Christ gives life to our spirits, our "house" continues to be temporary, flawed. Even as Jesus "tabernacled" among us, so we tent-camp now, in skin and bones that were made from dust and will return to dust.

Trapped in these earthly confines (2 Corinthians 5:2, 5), we long to receive our new resurrection bodies—to be clothed with Christ;

we ache to be free from our constant wrong choices and death-doings. Wordless groans express the deepest longings of our heart, without words to pray and beseech our God. And here, *here*, we see again God's sensitivity to us, His preparation for us, His desire to emancipate us. Even as God was not deaf to Israel's pleas, enslaved in Egypt, so He hears our groanings now: "And the sons of Israel sighed because of the bondage, and they cried out; and their cry for help because of their bondage rose up to God. So God heard their groaning; and God remembered His covenant with Abraham, Isaac, and Jacob" (Exodus 2:23–24).

The Scriptures comfort us: "The Spirit also helps our weakness; for we do not know how to pray as we should, but the Spirit himself intercedes for us with groanings too deep for words; and He who searches the hearts knows what the mind of the Spirit is, because He intercedes for the saints according to the will of God" (Romans 8:26–27).

We are not left groaning and trapped, enslaved in a body with no deliverance. No, though we are mute, the Spirit speaks for us; though we see no one standing between us, pleading for us, the Spirit interprets our longings before the throne.

Set Free

One glorious day, all creation will be set free from slavery to corruption into freedom (Romans 8:21). We saw a foreshadowing of this when Jesus on the cross "cried out again with a loud voice, and yielded up His spirit. And behold, the . . . earth shook; and the rocks were split, and the tombs were opened; and many bodies of the saints who had fallen asleep were raised" (Matthew 27:50–52). For a moment, Christ's groan set creation free, and the earth groaned and gave up the dead and acknowledged the Lord of all the universe.

Though we stand too often in darkness, in betrayal, in temptation; though we groan before the redemption of the earth and our own redemption as children of God, God sees us, even as He sees His beloved Son. Because the Christ of the Garden stands between us and God, and we are indeed complete in Him.

⌘ *Listen*

The joyful anticipation deepens. All around us we observe a pregnant creation. The difficult times of pain throughout the world are simply birth pangs. But it's not only around us; it is within us. The Spirit of God is arousing us within. We're also feeling the birth pangs. These sterile and barren bodies of ours are yearning for full deliverance. That is why waiting does not diminish us, any more than waiting diminishes a pregnant mother. We are enlarged in the waiting. We, of course, don't see what is enlarging us. But the longer we wait, the larger we become, and the more joyful our expectancy.

Meanwhile, the moment we get tired in the waiting, God's Spirit is right alongside helping us along. If we don't know how or what to pray, it doesn't matter. He does our praying in and for us, making prayer out of our wordless sighs, our aching groans. He knows us far better than we know ourselves . . . and keeps us present before God. That's why we can be so sure that every detail in our lives of love for God is working into something good.

Romans 8:22–28,
The Message

🞄 *Learn*

Our longing desires can no more exhaust the fulness of the Godhead, than our imagination can touch their measure.

George MacDonald,
Unspoken Sermons (Series One)

See every flower straighten its stalk, lift up its neck, and with outstretched head stand expectant: something more than the sun, greater than the light, is coming, is coming—none the less surely coming that is long upon the road! What matters today, or tomorrow, or ten thousand years to Life Himself, to Love Himself! He is coming, is coming, and the necks of all humanity are stretched out to see Him come!

George MacDonald,
Lilith

🞄 *Live*

✦ What are your deepest groanings? (They don't have to be deeply "spiritual.") When have you experienced the Holy Spirit groaning through you?

✦ Describe your greatest physical pain. Compare that anguish with the longing of creation for relief. What about your longings?

Four

SHAME IN THE GARDEN

I'm ashamed of you!" the mother exclaimed, eyebrows knitted together, a frown puckering her mouth. Her jaw clamped in a rigid line. "How could you do that?"

"Shame on you!" the father said by his actions, as he re-did the chores assigned to his child.

"Shameless!" we say of the brazen woman dressed seductively.

"You should be ashamed of yourself." "Aren't you ashamed of yourself?" "You never get it right." "Only a B? You should get A's." "Why aren't you earning more?" "Why didn't you get a different job?"

"Shame on me," we tell ourselves, working harder, or avoiding relationships, or losing ourselves in compulsive behavior.

Whether conveyed through words, tone, attitude, or posture, shame happens. It happens when we don't measure up, don't do something perfectly, and feel another's censure for our failure. We interpret it as a global personality problem, a defect in our being, and come to the conclusion not that we *made* a mistake, but that we *are* a mistake.

Shame entered the human race when Adam and Eve, having

eaten the only expressly forbidden fruit in the entire garden, covered themselves and hid from God. But throughout the Scriptures we find people who should be covered with shame but are not because they have recovered the freedom lost in Eden—freedom found only in the wholehearted embrace of God. "Those who looked to Him were radiant; their faces are never covered with shame" (Psalm 34:5 NIV). In our journey from Eden to Gethsemane, we will trace the trail of shame and look to Christ, who endured the cross, despising its shame . . . and learn new strategies for shame-less living.

14. SHAME IN EDEN

How does shame fit into this scenario? It doesn't. We can't imagine a more perfect setting; nor can we grasp the freedom Adam and Eve experienced in Eden. Though it lingers just outside the edges of our dreams, and we sense this perfection nearby, it evades us. Fresh-faced with wonder, they romped and tasted and enjoyed the very best life God could provide for them. The most exotic and elaborate garden in our world today wilts in comparison with Eden; it's a wonder Adam's and Eve's hearts didn't burst from the fullness of joy. And I have to ask—partly as a wanna-be gardener and partly because we have just come through one of the rainiest seasons in memory and every horizontal surface holds standing water filled with mosquito larvae—what was it like, a garden without mosquitoes? Adam and Eve had no worries in this area, or they wouldn't have walked around in the buff. The Scriptures recount in modest form their early experience in Eden: "And the man and his wife were both naked and were not ashamed" (Genesis 2:25).

Unless the Scriptures employ time-lapse techniques here, the clock has not moved forward much between their shame-free living and the Serpent's approach. The very next verse in Scripture hisses at us: "Now the serpent was more crafty than any beast of the field which the Lord God had made. And he said to the woman . . ." (Genesis 3:1). Warning drums sound in our head, like the ominous music from *Jaws*, pushing us to the edge of our seat and elevating our heart rate. "Watch out! Trouble ahead! Snake crossing!" we want to shout. Because we know this scene. We've watched the movie, read the book, have the lines memorized.

The scene we are about to watch is the first recorded incidence of shame.

Shame Defined

Shame, as we now know it, stands separate from the traditional dictionary definition of guilt. Humiliation, wanting to cringe into a tiny, invisible ball and self-destruct, is closer to the current meaning. Shame, according to Ronald and Patricia Potter-Efron, is "a painful belief in one's basic defectiveness as a human being."[1] Even knowing intellectually that we are loved by God in Christ Jesus does not always eliminate our base of shame. Shame exists both within and without the body of Christ and is a learned response to the messages of those around us.

Areas of Vulnerability

There is something amazing and astounding about Adam and Eve's ability to be naked and unashamed. I will never forget the image of one of my children standing on the bathroom counter, stark naked after a bath, smiling at the mirror image. *Smiling*. No one does that after the age of, say, five. Body shame traces back through the centuries like a slug leaving a tacky trail. We've heard stories of women bathing in the privacy of their own bathroom with a gown covering them, coached not to look at themselves naked or even in a mirror because the body was something to be avoided, a tool easily accessed by sin. The body is evil; don't look.

Horror stories return from gym class and the locker room, where the gym teacher stood at the shower door with a clipboard and class roster, placing a dark pencil check mark next to each person's name as they entered the shower. At least in the girls' locker room, the community shower was enough to cause death by mortification; better to be graded down and avoid the embarrassment of body comparison. The hideous Popeye gym suits of my childhood should have been sufficient for keeping students humble; the mandatory shower, however, struck students in their area of greatest embarrassment.

Most people who have survived life past toddlerhood are uncomfortable with nakedness—their own or another's. In the original Garden, then, it makes sense that Satan would slither into the picture at precisely the time Adam and Eve were unashamed of their nakedness. We have been embarrassed about our bodies ever since.

We become vulnerable when we love others, opening ourselves up to the possibility of shame. We become vulnerable, naked, when we attempt new things, risk attaining a dream, try to tell another truth in love. We become vulnerable when we ask for forgiveness, confessing to a darkness within or a failing. When we are vulnerable, we are easy game for the predator, shame.

Ironically, we also display our shame base when we make ourselves overly visible. It is possible, I think, that shame shows up both in embarrassment over our bodies *and*, in a perverse way, in a flaunting of our bodies. So that what some would call shameless behavior is actually a fighting against the voice of shame. The desperate near-nudity in our culture is actually revealing the essence of shame, which is separation from our identity in Christ.

While it looks like the opposite of the "Don't look at me—I'm naked" shame, it is really another side of the same coin, an attempt to appear acceptable on someone else's terms. Either extreme reveals our brokenness and separation from God.

Doubt

Working on the area of doubt, Satan is also a pro. He sidled up to Eve when she was vulnerable, unashamed, and then moved to a chink in her armor: "You sure God said that, honey? No, surely He didn't say that!" His words caused Eve to doubt both her memory and God's goodness. Doubt is a great shame inducer, making us wonder if something is wrong with us, with our memories. Whether we doubt ourselves, our God-given abilities, or God, we give Satan a free slide into the Garden.

The Serpent loves to inspire doubt and loves to twist the truth. With just his slight shifting of the words, Eve was hooked. "Indeed, has God said, 'You shall not eat from *any* tree of the garden'?" (Genesis 3:1, emphasis added). Shame tends to believe the other is always right and we are always wrong. I know, because that's my first instinct.

To wriggle away from the garden piranha, Eve could have refused to argue. This is a great strategy for parents, for people in conflict, for us. Don't get hooked into an argument or debate about a third party. Instead, send the whisperer, the doubter, to the original source. "Talk to God about that, Satan. He'll set you straight."

But we love to argue, and Eve somehow felt compelled to enter into a dialogue with this most beautiful and clever companion. Unfortunately, she chose to elaborate on God's original prohibition, which put her right into the enemy's clutches. Self-doubt, and the need to defend herself, kicked in, and she put words in God's mouth: "You shall not eat from it or touch it, lest you die" (Genesis 3:3). *Touch* wasn't prohibited, *eating* was.

Satan, the consummate deceiver, sows a little more doubt for good measure: "You surely shall not die!" (v. 4).

Eve believed his bold lie, and Adam believed Eve; they both ended up separated from their true identity in God. Their immediate response to God's calling them, after succumbing to temptation, was to hide and then cover themselves with leaves. Hiding when we feel shame is a common response. When we have been snared in a trap, found to be wrong, or are just being fresh-faced and honest, we easily embrace shame from others and from our own internal shame monitor.

God's response to Adam and Eve touches me. Yes, there is a consequence to their sin, but His first response is one of love and sacrifice. His sorrow and heartbreak over their choices and their loss of innocence are woven between the lines as He tenderly covers their nakedness with fur.

Still, we find ourselves, with them, cast out from Eden, stumbling around in shame, unable to accept His covering, unable to embrace the truth—that God loved us from the beginning and would rather die than have us separated from Him.

88 *Listen*

Fear not, for you will not be put to shame; neither feel humiliated, for you will not be disgraced; but you will forget the shame of your youth, and the reproach of your widowhood you will remember no more. For your husband is your Maker, whose name is the Lord of hosts; and your Redeemer is the Holy One of Israel, who is called the God of all the earth.

Isaiah 54:4–5

Learn

Shame entered the human drama as a result of sin. Broken fellowship with God meant broken fellowship with each other. Separation from God caused an internal separation and a relational separation. Adam and Eve were no longer true to their soulful selves, nor were they true to one another. "Shame is the expression of the fact that we no longer accept the other person as the gift of God," writes Dietrich Bonhoeffer. "In the unity of unbroken obedience man is naked in the presence of man, uncovered, revealing both body and soul, and yet he is not ashamed. Shame only comes into existence in the world of division." The root cause of shame is the unnatural, disobedient and dysfunctional violation of body and soul. Sin makes us terribly vulnerable, insecure and fundamentally dissatisfied with ourselves and others.

Douglas D. Webster,
Soulcraft: How God Shapes Us Through Relationships

Live

- When are you most susceptible to shame?
- Where do you hear shaming messages, and from whom? In what setting?
- What message do you hear from God regarding shame?

15. SHAME BETWEEN THE GARDENS

In a world that determines acceptability with a tape measure, IQ test, or bank statement, shame becomes a natural companion. Everywhere we turn, status symbols remind us of our failure to excel, our falling short of perfection. Tim felt ashamed and emasculated because, in spite of a master's degree, his pay as a minister prohibited him from buying a home for his family or driving a decent car. For Peter, shame hid itself in false bravado, in boasting and bragging about accomplishments and popularity. If he could only build himself up in the world's eyes, perhaps he could lose his high level of shame.

Whether we are comparing bust size or running times, offspring or investments, this is a game we cannot win. The cards are always stacked against us when we internalize the message that we are failures if we don't look or act or speak a certain way. Taken to its extreme, chronic shame hisses in our ear, *"You're a mistake. You should never have been born."* When we look to others for approval or identity, we live in a no-man's land, exiled from Eden but prohibited from entering into the benefits of Gethsemane.

We carry shame about our own inadequacies, failings, and mistakes. Shame also shows up when we connect another's actions or reputation to our own sense of worth. After ten years, Lucille finally recognized that she'd hauled shame around with her, like a truckload of compost, ever since her daughter's divorce. Divorce simply shouldn't happen in a Christian family, and somehow her daughter's failed marriage meant that Lucille had failed to raise her properly.

We carry shame over our past as well. Imperfect parents can unwittingly heap shame upon us; incorporating failures and mistakes into our personality and never relinquishing them to God can increase our shame. Pain from childhood—living with abuse, alcoholism or other addiction, neglect, abandonment, lies—settles like clay into the bottom of our hearts, stopping us from drinking in the love of God and working its way through our souls until we feel shame over issues and problems we didn't cause. Shame because we are different, because our homes were unsafe, because everyone else on earth but us lived a "normal" life.

We lug shame from the past into our families and pass shame down to the next generation when we continue to hide, and thus not deal with, the pain. The subjects no one is allowed to talk about are guns loaded with shame.

Shame increases in the presence of constant correction; we add to shame with our own compulsions and behavior. Shame rears its head in our homes and churches and communities and workplaces when we never allow ourselves to be wrong.

This parasite preys on our souls, sucking the very life from our relationships. It will keep us from trusting others, from developing close friendships, from real vulnerability. Shame will also keep us from experiencing real forgiveness in Christ.

Symptoms of Shame

Though we might not call it a disease, there are symptoms that alert us to the presence of shame. Watch for labels—people labeling us, or our labeling of another. "You're an idiot!" "What a loser." Name-calling in general can increase shame. One young mother introduced her rambunctious toddler as "my little monster" until she realized that such a name labeled him and could well cause him to grow into exactly that. Calling people, including ourselves, only names that edify is a discipline important to cultivate. Statements like "I'm ashamed of you" and "You should be ashamed of yourself" cannot be particularly helpful either. Other statements to avoid include "How dare you!" and "How could you?"

Here are additional signs that shame lurks like a snake—and not a harmless garden snake—in the weeds, waiting to overcome us. Symptoms of shame include:

- ✦ Anger
- ✦ Boasting
- ✦ Blaming
- ✦ Perfectionism
- ✦ Defensiveness
- ✦ Edginess
- ✦ Fatigue
- ✦ Underachieving
- ✦ Poor self-care

A Tool for Growth

Shame becomes helpful when it flags our attention, so we examine the messages of others and our own internal whisperings: *You don't measure up. You're a failure. A mistake. Worthless. Your body is inadequate, defective, below average.* Hear what the *shoulds* say: *You should earn more money so you can prove yourself worthy. You should keep a cleaner house, be unfailingly kind and polite, cross off everything on the to-do list; you should drive a better car, have children who are model citizens, earn your parents' approval. You should have unlimited funds, be able to function without sleep, and smile at all times. You should never be upset, angry, or anything but sweet.*

These are the whisperings of shame, the voice of the Serpent, who ever seeks to separate us from the love of God, the adequacy of Christ, the perfection of His covering.

Used appropriately, shame can show us where we can grow, where we need to laugh, where we are safe or unsafe in relationships. Tim, for instance, ashamed because of his inability to provide better for his family, picked up on the shame, turning it into a tool for growth. He determined to use his financial state as a time to learn humility, to identify with the poorer people in his community, and to teach himself and his children to detach their self-worth from their possessions. Albert Camus said, "What doesn't kill you makes you strong." So we listen to the niggling voice because it teaches us where we can trust God more, where we can learn anew to rely on Christ's accomplishment on our behalf.

We listen, and we look to Gethsemane for Christ's strategy in handling shame.

88 *Listen*

The Lord your God is in your midst, a victorious warrior. He will exult over you with joy, He will be quiet in His love, He will rejoice over you with shouts of joy.... Behold, I am going to deal at that time with all your oppressors, I will save the lame and gather the outcast, and I will turn their shame into praise and renown in all the earth.

Zephaniah 3:17, 19

88 *Learn*

Without an exception, all addictions are based on shame. *People become addicted to a substance or to an activity as a way of dealing with or covering up their shame. Every person who suffers from an addiction carries an enormous—although often secret—burden of shame. For that reason, whenever shame is present addiction is predictable.*

Drs. Hemfelt, Minirth, and Meier,
We Are Driven

88 *Live*

✦ What symptoms of shame do you notice in your own life? In the lives of people you love?
✦ Where does it primarily originate?
✦ When has shame become a tool for growth?

16. SHAME IN THE SECOND GARDEN: GETHSEMANE

Studying the Scriptures, my heart lurched when I read, and re-read, Hebrews 12:2: ". . . fixing our eyes on Jesus, the author and perfecter of faith, who for the joy set before Him endured the cross, *despising the shame*, and has sat down at the right hand of the throne of God" (emphasis added). Christ understood shame in a far deeper way than we will ever experience—shame in relationship to the cross and to His true identity.

Christ knew the Scripture, "Cursed is everyone who hangs on a tree" (Galatians 3:13; Deuteronomy 21:23). Typically in Old Testament times, hanging was not a means of death but a sequel to death. Hanging on a crude wooden beam or post or tree "exposed the corpse to ultimate disgrace," according to Charles Ryrie.[2] Christ knew this, but somehow "despised the shame" of the cross. The ultimate shame of the cross was that it labeled Christ as a sinner separated from God.

Here, the word for shame comes from a term meaning *disfigurement*, leading us to see ourselves as deformed, hideous. Shame also has its roots in a word for *dishonest*, and this is the ultimate dishonesty: that the holy Son of God would be charged as a criminal and hung on a cross to die. Yet He gladly took the disfiguring label of criminal, of sinner, for our sakes, that we might never again be separated from Him.

In our own world, shame is also a dishonesty: shame lies to us, telling us we are defective, problematic, a mistake. But Christ stands against this lie with His life, His death, and His promise to love us. Looking at Hebrews 2:11, we find that Christ is not *ashamed* to call us His family. In fact, the prospect of bringing us into His family filled Him with joy—"the joy set before Him" (12:2)—and allowed Him to endure the cross and despise its shame.

Christ knew who He was and refused to allow shame to disfigure Him or dissuade Him from His purpose.

Looking at Christ, we are changed. When we move into His presence and are held in His loving embrace, shame dissipates, like fog in sunshine, in the white light of His love.

88 *Listen*

Those who look to him are radiant; their faces are never covered with shame.

Psalm 34:5 NIV

88 *Learn*

Shame feelings should lead us to God, who never covers us with shame, but instead covers us with Jesus Christ. 'Put on Christ.' Cover yourself with Christ, the Christ who endured the cross but stood against the disfigurement of the cross's reputation.

Shame can lead us to dishonesty, a covering up of truth. See what Adam and Eve did immediately upon realizing how suddenly far they were from their ideal, their creation in God's image? Shame defaces us so we no longer know our own value, who we are. But when we realize that we are the beloved, our shame level drops.

Why? Because we learn, in the presence of Christ, that "there is therefore now no condemnation for those who are in Christ Jesus" (Romans 8:1).

Jane Rubietta

88 *Live*

✦ What moves you about Christ's enduring the cross, despising the shame?
✦ How often is shame a factor that keeps you from Christ?
✦ How do you think Christ feels about you, your shame, your soul?

17. GARDEN LIVING:
SHAME-LESS STRATEGIES

How do we stand against, rein in, strongly oppose feelings of shame? The word for *despise* in Hebrews 12:2 means just that. Christ strongly opposed, stood against, the shame of the cross. Here are some strategies to use that we might not be disfigured by shame, but that, looking to Him, our faces might be radiant:

- *Stand in grace:* In 2 Samuel 22:17–20, God rescues David because He delights in him. Listen to the voice of God delighting in you, and let Him rescue you from shame.
- *Rejoice in hope:* When we, in hope, cling to Christ, tenacious as climbing ivy, we will never be disappointed (Romans 5:1–5).
- *Refuse to listen:* Eve didn't turn her back on the Serpent, but we can, once we recognize his voice. To turn away from the hiss of shame, we must . . .
- *Examine and dispel the shame:* Look for truth hidden in the curse. For instance, if you always come away from an interaction with a certain person feeling a sense of shame, the message is clear: that relationship isn't safe. What can be done to create safety, then, in that relationship?
- *Exchange the lies for truth:* "I am fearfully and wonderfully made; wonderful are Thy works, and my soul knows it very well" (Psalm 139:14).
- *Look to God:* "In you, O Lord, I have taken refuge. Let me never be put to shame" (Psalm 71:1 NIV).
- *Know the inheritance:* "Instead of their shame my people will receive a double portion, and instead of disgrace they will rejoice in their inheritance" (Isaiah 61:7 NIV).

❌ *Listen*

. . . the Lord your God . . . has worked wonders for you; never again will my people be shamed. Then you will know that I am in Israel, that I am

the Lord your God, and that there is no other; never again will my people be shamed.

Joel 2:26–27 NIV

⊞ *Learn*

When we are set free from shame, an interesting phenomenon happens in community. When we can be real before God, we can ultimately find acceptance and love. We are free to be wrong, to be vulnerable; we no longer have to be perfect. Church becomes, then, a safe place, a refuge for others. They are drawn in. "Hey, she has pain, but look at her love! God did that? I want to know that love, that God." How amazing, that Christ turns our shame and failure into a tool for reaching others! Yet again, Christ has the final say in the battle with the Serpent.

Jane Rubietta

⊞ *Live*

+ How do you resist shame? What tools can you employ to stand against its deforming power?
+ How do you give grace, embrace others in the loving acceptance of God, and resist the temptation to shame another?

Five

SACRIFICE IN THE GARDEN

Crammed into a small plane seat as a fresh-from-college graduate, I pored over the opening chapters of the Bible, reading and underlining and then stopping to cry. Christ's sacrifice was foretold in the Garden of Eden! From the very beginning, the Trinity made plans to redeem human beings from their fallen state. What amazing love: this just-made world, crafted so beautifully and with such tenderness for us, and so quickly brought to bear the curse of our fallenness. Even then, Christ planned to give up heaven, to come to earth, to offer up the final sacrifice for our sin. My heart stumbles over this truth; stumbled then, as a young adult; stumbles now, as a less-young adult.

I recognized my own patterns in Adam and Eve's cover-up for sin, the first pathetic human attempt at looking good in another's sight—and God's. Tracing the sacrifices from Eden through the Old Testament, learning that they ended with Christ at Gethsemane, moved me deeply and nestled into the subterranean layers of my mind and heart. Even now, pouring over the Scriptures and zooming through history all the way to my own life, God's sacrificial love brings me to my knees in worship.

18. SACRIFICE IN EDEN

Adam and Eve's Sacrifice

Adam and Eve's story is one of selfishness, of grasping for control and glory and godlike power. But sacrifice is part of the scene as well. They sacrificed—gave up, relinquished, exchanged—the life in Eden for something that looked better. Tarnished, jaded, self-serving, their idea of a covering for their sin was more a cover-up: hurriedly ripping leaves off fig trees in order to hide. Most sobering, they sacrificed their relationship with God, allowing the world and all its temptations to come between them, to usurp His place in their souls and lives. In Eden began the reign of self, and to this day it is our greatest temptation, and perhaps the root of our sinful acts.

Adam and Eve's idea of atonement—of covering for their sin—was deficient: cold, bloodless leaves did nothing to reestablish their relationship with God or cleanse their hearts from the ugliness of their sin. Their inadequate and imperfect sacrifice glared in light of God's next move, His sacrifice.

A sacrifice, to be a real sacrifice, cannot be self-serving; God sacrificed with forethought and thoroughness, assuring that their covering was competent, the sacrifice sufficient.

God's Sacrifice

Even in the midst of the damaging and hurtful betrayal of His treasured children, God's forgiving, redemptive love enfolds them.

"And the Lord God made garments of skin for Adam and his wife, and clothed them" (Genesis 3:21). Not until later do we learn that "without the shedding of blood there is no sacrifice for sin." But God, in grace, foreshadowed the coming sacrificial system and the ultimate sacrifice of His Son, Christ, when He killed the animals and covered Adam and Eve, not with leaves, but with fur, from the first of His creation.

God's sacrifices go much deeper than skinning a couple of animals, however. He sacrificed—gave up, relinquished, exchanged—His desire and right for first place in our lives. He wanted—still wants—to be the perfect lover, the all-consuming passion, of His creation, and yet gave up the right to control or domineer us. This lover allowed them, and allows us, to choose to love Him. Speaking as a parent myself, I can only imagine the cost involved for our God.

God also, in the Garden so long ago, gave up His dreams for our very best—the perfect life—and gave us the option of returning on our own to Him. And then, in an act of great compassion, relinquished judgment, exchanging it for mercy, and presented us with the possibility of coming home.

How God's heart must have bled as He sacrificed the animals in the Garden, and yet God's parent-heart longed for His kids, for their wholeness, for their love. And so He exchanged the life of the animals for the life of His people.

88 *Listen*

Surely the arm of the Lord is not too short to save, nor his ear too dull to hear. But your iniquities have separated you from your God; your sins have hidden his face from you, so that he will not hear. . . .

The Lord looked and was displeased that there was no justice. He saw that there was no one, he was appalled that there was no one to intervene; so his own arm worked salvation for him, and his own righteousness sustained him.

Isaiah 59:1–2, 15b–16 NIV

⊞ *Learn*

I stand amazed in the presence of Jesus the Nazarene,
And wonder how he could love me, a sinner, condemned, unclean.

For me it was in the garden he prayed: "Not my will, but thine."
He had no tears for his own griefs, but sweat-drops of blood for mine.

In pity angels beheld him, and came from the world of light
To comfort him in the sorrows he bore for my soul that night.

He took my sins and my sorrows, he made them his very own;
He bore the burden to Calvary, and suffered and died alone.

When with the ransomed in glory his face I at last shall see,
'twill be my joy through the ages to sing of his love for me.

Charles Gabriel,
"I Stand Amazed in the Presence"

⊞ *Live*

+ When has an action of yours caused another to sacrifice?
+ How do you cover over your sins, mistakes, failures?
+ What has God done to bring you back to Him?

19. BETWEEN TWO GARDENS:
THE SACRIFICIAL SYSTEM

Following the eviction from Eden, we find the famous first off-spring offering up their own sacrifices: one of veggies, another of meat. Rather than examining whether the offering itself was deficient or God is really picky, we must go instead to the heart of the one offering the sacrifice. Competition, covetousness, and a selfish interest in his own well-being fill Cain's heart. "What, you think I'm gonna look after my brother?" Perhaps nothing at all was wrong with the grain offering Cain sacrificed to God. Darkness, however, filled him, and God saw it.

Sacrifice has more to do with the state of our heart than the value of the offering itself. Sacrifices demonstrate not our wealth, but the depth of our love. Still, in a world where the visible is valued, and the bigger the better (house, car, salary, body part . . .) we easily pervert the idea of sacrifice. If it makes us look good or somehow covers up our failings, we go for it, long for it, buy it, offer it, and clang cymbals along the way to make sure it's noticed.

Just prior to exiting Egypt, the Israelites eat a Passover dinner, including bread without leaven (leaven being a symbol for sin) and a perfect lamb without spot or blemish, whose blood covered the doorframes and signaled that the angel of death would pass over those dwelling within. That covering of blood saved the Israelites from death.

Throughout the Old Testament, after God instituted the

sacrificial system, a complex system of various offerings designed to help us move back into relationship with God, we hear refrains of "I desire obedience and not sacrifice." Why? Because a sacrifice is a giving back, an offering of joy and thanksgiving and repentance and sorrow and fellowship. The word offering has as its root meaning "to draw near," and our offerings, our sacrifices, should be just that: given out of a loving desire to draw near to God. But the Israelites turned this gracious opportunity to love God and restore their relationship with Him into an ugly attempt to buy God's favor, to look good in another's eyes, to secure social standing and political correctness. We, like the Israelites, may use sacrifices as a magic panacea, a "Sunday-morning-after" solution to a week, or a life, of wantonness and idolatry. Yes, God wants obedience that flows out of love!

We, too, use the system. Our attempts at sacrifice, like the Israelites', are wretchedly incomplete, covered with the soot of impure motives, corrupted by vanity.

Perhaps we unintentionally sacrifice our family, marriage, friends, gifts, and dreams to the all-consuming job, debt, or even hobby. Or we view the "system" of religious rightness as a balance scale, where this "sacrifice" (time, money, attendance at church, charitable work, committees) is an atonement, a means of covering up our failure to meet God's standards. We live in constant motion to avoid facing the truth: None of our sacrifices make us whole.

Just as Adam and Eve's sacrifice—their covering, their atonement—would wither and fall off, so do our sacrifices, our attempts to buy merit and cover up our deficiencies and failings; they wither and crumple and eventually reveal that which we wanted so desperately to camouflage: our failings and our sins, which ever separate us from God. We cannot clothe ourselves with good works, for in the bright light of God's holiness they are filthy rags. We cannot complete ourselves. We can only be complete, and completely covered, with the sacrifice of One, the perfect sacrifice that clothes us, cleanses us, completes us.

All our works, then, are to proceed as gifts from us to God for the glory of God. They are never to be attempts at looking good, though frequently God reminds me that I seek too often my own glory and not His, or that my desires are split between the two.

Once this week, as fear and weariness again filled my bones with lead and my spirit with clouds, I wondered if my state of constant depletion glorifies God. Does it appeal to Him, like some offering or sacrifice, a fragrant aroma? I doubt it. Fear and fatigue do not make God look good. We think of these as altruistic; America applauds hard work and its resultant exhaustion. These become, or seem to become, a great sacrifice. But in reality, they call into question whether God truly is all-powerful, all-knowing, all-present if I find it necessary to work endlessly and rarely sleep my fill, snapping at everyone because my control is frayed to the last thread and fear gnaws even that strand.

So what I like to think of as sacrificial living is actually self-centered. It harms me, my family, and my relationship with God.

A real sacrifice, instead, puts the focus on God. And this leads us to the ultimate and final and only true sacrifice for our sins. It leads us to the Garden, to Gethsemane and to Golgotha and to the empty tomb.

⌘ *Listen*

This is how much God loved the world: He gave his Son, his one and only Son. And this is why: so that no one need be destroyed; by believing in him, anyone can have a whole and lasting life. God didn't go to all the trouble of sending his Son merely to point an accusing finger, telling the world how bad it was. He came to help, to put the world right again. Anyone who trusts in him is acquitted; anyone who refuses to trust him has long since been under the death sentence without knowing it.

John 3:16–18
The Message

88 *Learn*

When Christ calls a man, he bids him come and die.

Dietrich Bonhoeffer

88 *Live*

+ What superficial sacrifices have you offered?
+ How are they self-centered?
+ What is at the root of such a sacrifice? (e.g. fear, perfectionism, workaholism, self-righteousness . . .) Can you excavate those roots with the God of all mercy, the gracious Gardener?

20. The Final Sacrifice

What can be said about Christ's sacrifice without trivializing it? The most profound and complete work ever done on behalf of a human being, since God created us in His image, was done by Christ. Theologians spend entire lives thinking about the sacrifice of Jesus Christ. A quick book search by subject reveals more than five thousand books about Jesus available to us. How can these few pages cover the depth and breadth of such an enormous, mysterious, profound topic?

Can we even begin to grasp what it means for the Almighty God to leave heaven and come to earth? And as a baby, no less? And then the baby grows up into a Man who is still God but lays aside His God-hood and lives just like we do, only perfectly, and then dies for us. And this Man, who presents himself as a sacrifice for us, fulfills the entire sacrificial system set up in the Old Testament, a system based on farm animals and agriculture.

No one has ever done anything like this in all of human history. It is beyond my fragile ability to form words and sentences; it fills my head and my heart so full that I cannot think. In fact, even as I dwell on these facts, the immense love of God, of Jesus Christ, for me overwhelms me and tears puddle in my eyes. No one has ever loved me like this before. No one can ever love you like this, except for God.

His sacrifice began in Eden, as He prepared even then to come in the flesh, to live life shaped like us, that we might be restored to the image of God. Christ sacrificed His place in heaven, gave up all the rights of His deity, and "emptied Himself" (Philippians 2:7). By "being found in appearance as a man" (Philippians 2:8 NIV), Christ did what we could not do for ourselves. Assuming human flesh, He set about living the life God had designed for us: a life of total reliance on God. Adam and Eve could not, would not live in this way, and so Christ took our frame and lived it for us, in our place. He, though tempted in all ways as we are, remained sinless, perfect. He not only comes to our aid when tempted, but He fulfilled all the demands of the perfection-seeking law.

Look with me for a moment at the sacrifices in the Old Testament.[1] Christ has fulfilled every single one of them.

✦ *The Burnt Offering:* This offering was a voluntary act of worship; an atonement for unintentional sin in general; an expression of devotion, commitment, and complete surrender to God. In Gethsemane, Jesus said, "Not My will, but Thine be done" (Luke 22:42).

✦ *The Grain Offering:* "I am the bread of life" (John 6:35).

✦ *The Peace Offering:* "He Himself is our peace" (Ephesians 2:14).

✦ *The Sin Offering and the Trespass Offering:* Both were fulfilled by the perfect, sinless life of Christ: "He committed no sin, and no deceit was found in his mouth. . . . He himself bore our sins in his body on the tree, so that we might die to sins and live for righteousness; by his wounds you have been healed" (1 Peter 2:22, 24 NIV; see also Isaiah 53:10).

✦ *The Drink Offering:* "If any man is thirsty, let him come to Me and drink." "Whoever drinks of the water that I give him shall never thirst; but the water . . . shall become in him a well of water springing up to eternal life" (John 7:37; John 4:14). "He poured out Himself to death" (Isaiah 53:12).

We could further examine the timing: Christ was crucified at the exact moment of the morning sacrifice in the temple, and He died at the precise time of the evening sacrifice. And the Passover supper? Christ became that perfect Lamb, without spot or blemish. "Behold, the Lamb of God who takes away the sin of the world!" (John 1:29).

We could continue with the feasts in the Scriptures, and marvel at how Christ's crucifixion, death, and resurrection coincide with all the feasts except the Feast of Trumpets (the Lord will return with a blast of trumpets!). We could look at Abraham's covenant with God, when God agreed that He would keep His part of the bargain and human beings would keep theirs; and how God not only kept His side, He sent His Son to keep the human side.

Yes, we can look at all these remarkable examples of Christ's fulfillment by His own sacrifice. And if, after all this, our hearts are not moved by His love for us, if we are not on the floor bowed in worship, if sacrifices of praise and thanksgiving do not flow from our lips . . .

"It is finished." We can add nothing to the sacrifice. There no longer remains any sacrifice for our sin. With the shedding of Christ's blood, His sinless life became the only possible atonement for sin. Jesus, the Messiah, did what we cannot do. And now He stands between us and God, ever covering us with himself, the perfect covering, the perfect clothing. The perfect sacrifice.

❁ *Listen*

[Christ said,] "sacrifices and offerings, burnt offerings and sin offerings you did not desire, nor were you pleased with them" (although the law required them to be made). Then he said, "Here I am, I have come to do your will." He sets aside the first to establish the second. And by that will, we have been made holy through the sacrifice of the body of Jesus Christ once for all.

Day after day every priest stands and performs his religious duties; again and again he offers the same sacrifices, which can never take away sins. But when this priest had offered for all time one sacrifice for sins, he sat down at the right hand of God. Since that time he waits for his enemies to be made his footstool, because by one sacrifice he has made perfect forever those who are being made holy.

Hebrews 10:8–14 NIV

⋈ *Learn*

We offer the world and ourselves to God. But we do it in Christ *and* in remembrance of Him. *We do it in Christ because He has already offered all that is to be offered to God. . . . In Him was* Life—and *this Life of all of us, He gave to God. . . . And we do it in remembrance of* Him *because, as we offer again and again our life and our world to God, we discover each time that there is nothing else to be offered but Christ Himself—the Life of the world, the fullness of all that exists. We come again and again with our lives to offer; we bring and "sacrifice"—that is, give to God—what He has given us; and each time we come to the* End *of all sacrifices, of all offerings . . . because each time it is revealed to us that Christ has* offered *all that exists, and that He and all that exists has been offered in His offering of Himself.*

Alexander Schmemann,
For the Life of the World

⋈ *Live*

✦ How does it feel to need a sacrifice and to know what Christ did for you, personally?

✦ Take time, in silence, to meditate on Christ's sacrifice for you.

21. Our Sacrifices Today

With Christ's death and resurrection, God abolished the sacrificial system instituted in the Garden of Eden. Sacrifices cannot save us any longer; there no longer remains any sacrifice for our sin.

What remains, then, for us? Are the sacrifices over?

A favorite hymn, "My Hope Is Built," gloriously trumpets the words, "dressed in His righteousness alone, faultless to stand before the throne." Phrases such as these adorn the New Testament: "put on Christ," "clothe yourselves with Christ." Reminiscent of Adam and Eve when they "put on" leaves—of God when He clothed them with warm fur, such phrases prod our conscience—we cannot buy, sell, bleed, work, or atone for our faults and failings; we can no longer cover them over with our good deeds and pious living. Instead, Christ has once and for all completed our need for covering.

Sacrifice implies an exchange—and it is not a sacrifice unless we value what is being given up. "I don't care, I didn't like it anyway," a teenager says about what seemed a generous giving away of an expensive article of clothing. Where there's no cost or value to the giver, there's no sacrifice.

A Widow's Mite/A Mighty Widow

The widow, with her gnarled hands and ancient face and timeless faith, sacrificed everything when she put her "mite" in the offering. In an age when women were not supposed to work, a widow was entirely at society's mercy. She had no means of support unless her family provided for her.

Did she waver with her fingertips over the slot in the box? Did she wrestle with her need for money and security, however minuscule that money might be, and her love for God? What happened inside her when she pinched the two pitiful coins between her work-worn fingertips, and then relinquished them?

And to drop them into the offering spout at the temple. This truly required faith on her part. The story in Mark 12 really begins in verse 38, when Jesus warns His followers about the religious elite: "Beware of the scribes . . . who devour widows' houses, and for appearance's sake offer long prayers; these will receive greater condemnation" (vv. 38, 40). Then Christ takes a seat opposite the treasury, and watches, and redefines sacrifice with the widow's story. Her sacrifice was all the more heartfelt and real because she knew that the religious bureaucrats "devoured widows' houses." And yet still she gave all she had, the ultimate sacrifice. How could she offer this sacrifice in light of the flagrant injustice and hypocrisy?

Because she saw beyond their posturing and impostering to the core, to the God whose love never left her, even when her husband died, even when the only things between her and absolute destitution were two tiny circles of copper, worth less than a penny.

Paul's words from Philippians 3:7–9 come to mind:

> But whatever things were gain to me, those things I have counted as loss for the sake of Christ. More than that, I count all things to be loss in view of the surpassing value of knowing Christ Jesus my Lord, for whom I have suffered the loss of all things, and count them but rubbish in order that I may gain Christ, and may be found in Him, not having a righteousness of my own derived from the Law, but that which is through faith in Christ, the righteousness which comes from God on the basis of faith.

With any sacrifice, we face a relinquishment moment: when we hold up the costs of an act or an item, and then give it up. In sacrifice, not only must something be given in exchange for something else, there is that moment of weigh-in, when we acknowledge the value of our sacrifice. How dearly do we hold this? What is this worth to me?

And then we die to it. We offer it on the altar in order for some-thing else to grow or come to life or fruition or realization. Sacrifice, seen in this way, is not unlike forgiveness, being willing to bear the cost, pay the price. Archbishop Fulton J. Sheen writes,

> Love is capable of overruling, in some way, your natural feel-ings about pain; that some things which otherwise might be painful are a joy to you when you find they benefit others. . . . Love is the only force in the world which can make pain beara-ble, and it makes it more than bearable by transforming it into the joy of sacrifice. . . . The deeper our love, the less the sense of pain, and the keener our joy of sacrifice.[2]

This does not mean that we do not gain when we sacrifice; only that our gain is not the point of the sacrifice (for then it is not a sacrifice!). We do gain, in fact. We gain the amazing knowledge that God is well pleased with us; that we have been obedient to His call on our lives for that moment; that our offering becomes a fragrant aroma to Him. And we are led to praise, and to thanksgiving, and to joy in the presence of God.

Whether another ever sees our giving, comments on it, benefits from it, God sees. God knows the cost involved, knows our hearts, and swoops in to fill us even more fully with himself. When we give sacrificially, we become more and more conformed to the image of Christ.

Sacrifices Today

Searching the Scriptures, I was delighted to find that our sacri-fices today, though they do not secure the state of our soul, bring

God glory. They begin with and in the heart: "Thou dost not delight in sacrifice, otherwise I would give it; Thou art not pleased with burnt offering. The sacrifices of God are a broken spirit; a broken and contrite heart, O God, Thou wilt not despise" (Psalm 51:16–17). Other sacrifices for us today:

✦ *Present your bodies a living sacrifice*—Romans 12:1—Giving up my life—presenting my body as a living sacrifice—means giving all of myself into God's hands and letting Him put me in the right place at the right time. Choosing to listen, and grow, and give up becomes a love offering to God.

✦ *Sacrifice of praise*—Hebrews 13:15, Jeremiah 17:26—Our sacrifices consist of praise, of lifting up our hands, also a relinquishment. "May the lifting up of my hands be like the evening sacrifice" (Psalm 141:2 NIV).

✦ *Sacrifice of Obedience*—1 Samuel 15:22—God no longer delights in burnt offerings and sacrifices: He delights in our obedience. We show our love by the way we live.

✦ *Sacrifice of Thanksgiving*—Psalm 116:17; 107:22—How is thanksgiving a sacrifice? It forces us to pull our eyes away from our own sufficiency, it changes our hearts, and it refocuses us on God. It's hard to be selfish and thankful at the same time!

Sacrifices of joy, of righteousness, of doing good and sharing—these sacrifices please God. God desires, yes, a broken and contrite heart, a heart that is broken and then filled with love that overflows in a lifestyle of love and mercy and justice. God doesn't, after all, want cold-blooded killing on an altar. He wants a relationship with us, one that is guaranteed by the sacrifice of His only Son.

With Christ's once-for-all sacrifice, the cuffs on our wrists spring open: we are set free. Free from scrambling to balance the scale, free from the chains of trying to look good, be good enough, measure up. The prison doors fly off the hinges and we emerge with a heart spilled over with the only remaining sacrifices: thanksgiving, praise, and obedience born from the life-changing love of Christ for us.

"Through Him then, let us continually offer up a sacrifice of praise to God, that is, the fruit of lips that give thanks to His name. And do not neglect doing good and sharing; for with such sacrifices God is pleased" (Hebrews 13:15–16).

And finally we understand what it means to be clothed with Christ.

⊠ *Listen*

I have been crucified with Christ; and it is no longer I who live, but Christ lives in me; and the life which I now live in the flesh I live by faith in the Son of God, who loved me, and delivered Himself up for me.

Galatians 2:20

For the love of Christ controls us, having concluded this, that one died for all, therefore all died; and He died for all, that they who live should no longer live for themselves, but for Him who died and rose again on their behalf.

2 Corinthians 5:14–15

⊠ *Learn*

My hope is built on nothing less than Jesus' blood and righteousness. I dare not trust the sweetest frame, but wholly lean on Jesus' name.

His oath, his covenant, his blood support me in the whelming flood. When all around my soul gives way, he then is all my hope and stay.

When he shall come with trumpet sound, O may I then in him be found!
Dressed in His righteousness alone, faultless to stand before the throne!

Chorus:
On Christ the solid rock I stand, all other ground is sinking sand;
All other ground is sinking sand.

Edward Mote,
"My Hope is Built"

⌘ *Live*

✦ Which sacrifices come naturally to you? In which areas do you desire to grow?

✦ When have you offered, out of obedience, a sacrifice of praise and then found your heart changed?

Six

THORNS IN THE GARDEN

I n one section of our yard, a once-wonderful stone pond re-
sides. Several trees, planted thoughtfully around the area,
shelter and provide shade, berries for birds, and cedar for
scent. A pipe runs underground into the basin to allow for
fish. Contour, texture, and height offer the possibility of creating a gorgeous setting, with rock-sprawling flowers like creeping
phlox and shade-loving varieties of other plants.

Note the phrase, "offer the possibility of creating a gorgeous
setting." This is in a perfect world. A world where someone tends
the overgrowth more than once a year. This summer, I picked one
of the hottest, most humid days in Chicago-land's schizophrenic
weather-calendar to approach the pond area. I would have avoided
it entirely, except that the hedges nearby along the fence line were
scratching the side of our car every time we exited the driveway.

Thistles with trunks like cornstalks encroached on the grass,
vying for my unprotected skin and embedding themselves in my
bare feet. Mosquitoes swarmed and attacked. Choking vines hung
off the tops of the trees, taunting me from their high perches. New
weed-trees had taken root and grown several feet. Horrified, I

rushed inside for long sleeves, jeans, shoes, thistle-proof gloves (which don't exist, I learned), and enough bug repellent to repulse a battalion of bugs. By the time I quit for the night—forced inside because of the pitch darkness surrounding me—every inch of cloth was drenched with sweat. I have disliked heat and its companion, sweat, since infancy and heat rash and high fevers that spiraled in seconds. Frankly, I find no real virtue in sweat and easily regard it as an offspring of the earliest Garden problems.

Wagonloads of weeds later, I have scarcely made a dent in the thriving jungle. Here and there, ground appears, freed of weeds so that the trees can breathe and receive rain. But the runners from the thistles also shoot around underground, popping up and multiplying exponentially. Scratches line my wrists and forearms, and itching bumps where the poison from the thistles invaded my skin remind me of the original curse. This land clearly produces thorns and this-tles, but the designer would have been horrified at its current state. This was not the blueprint the former owners drew up.

It is, however, a picture of my life—not the life the original De-signer intended. The soil of my soul becomes fertile land for every seed possible, and yet, without tending, undoubtedly bears thorns and thistles. The jungle state of my spirit is a far fall from God's initial desire.

The curse came in after Adam and Eve ripped the fruit from the tree and tore their hearts away from dependence on God. God's word to Adam, as a consequence of their disobedience, is seen in Genesis 3:17–19: "Cursed is the ground because of you; in toil you shall eat of it all the days of your life. Both thorns and thistles it shall grow for you; and you shall eat the plants of the field; by the sweat of your face you shall eat bread, till you return to the ground."

Sweat, bread, thorns—we will examine this trilogy as we move between the Gardens.

22. SWEAT IN THE GARDEN

Eden

Although teenagers might disagree, with their huge sleep needs and a metabolism that cannot keep pace with growth spurts, work is not a curse! Work existed in Eden before Adam and Eve reached for the forbidden fruit. Adam's job description was clear. "Then the Lord God took the man and put him into the garden of Eden to cultivate it and keep it" (Genesis 2:15). While we may dislike our particular job, work has been part of the picture since Creation.

The Scriptures read, "Cursed is the ground because of you; in toil you shall eat of it all the days of your life" (Genesis 3:17). Embedded in the Hebrew word for "toil" are the adjectives "worrisome, grievous, painful," whereas the word in Genesis 2:15 for "cultivate" generally means "to work or till." "By the sweat of your brow" describes the process of wresting a living from the land, the difficulty—sweat—involved in moving from grain in the field to enjoying food on the table. (This deduction comes easily for me.) Sweat, a picture of the strain of tending the land, is the curse, not the tending itself. We would fight the soil and the condition of work for all our earthly lives.

God had already planted the Garden; fruit swung heavily from the trees. Food in abundance surrounded them. But since Adam and

Eve took matters into their own hands, *they* would be responsible for the labor and the now-back-breaking work of tending the land. In a paradise where there had been no sweat Adam and Eve would now scrabble to keep up with the demands of a tedious job.

Between Two Gardens

Even after Eden's gates closed and the angel stood guard; even after the curse went into effect, we find God directing His people into a land where all the work was already done for them! He carefully provided a land where the ground was tilled and planted, where vines groaned with grapes that grew large as grapefruits. "I gave you houses you did not build and fields you did not plant," God reminded the Israelites (paraphrased, see Deuteronomy 6:10–12). But the people forgot God's good provision for them; they grew lax in their love of God, and strayed, and were sent into captivity because they refused to follow God. They kept working the land despite the Lord's assurance that He would provide for them if they honored Him with the first of the fruits of harvest, if they took one day off per week from their work to rest in His presence and provision, if they took one year off out of every seven to let the land recuperate and to replenish their own trust levels. And so, because they kept working and quit trusting, the people would be exiled from their land, taken into captivity, for seventy years. Seventy years later, with the land deeply rested, they would certainly tend and toil the neglected property!

Work becomes a curse by feeding our addictive tendencies to put something else in the place of God, and work has just enough positive reinforcement to make us work hard. It also fits snugly into the slot designed for trust. Our inclination since the Fall is to rely upon ourselves, and work is one more way we do this. Thus, the sweat of our brow—the difficulty and inherent benefits of hard work—constantly puts us in a quandary: in whom will we trust?

Just as God reminded the Israelites, the Lord nudges us, "You must deny yourselves and do no work." He commands us to step back and away from work, to take a break and let Him be in charge, handle the controls. We find this more difficult than the work itself, because then we must battle our compulsion to earn our way, be independent, self-made.

Part of the work curse, as well, is that we are then tempted to focus on the wrong riches. We look at the paycheck, line it up against the bills, and then punch in on the time clock because it's just not enough to cover us. Yet, in Ephesians 3:14–19, the Lord urges us to get it straight: Paul prays that God would grant us,

> . . . according to the riches of His glory, to be strengthened with power through His Spirit in the inner man; so that Christ may dwell in your hearts through faith; and that you, being rooted and grounded in love, may be able to comprehend with all the saints what is the breadth and length and height and depth, and to know the love of Christ which surpasses knowledge, that you may be filled up to all the fulness of God.

If we move back to the section in Genesis where the Serpent tempts Adam and Eve, he entices them with the promise of godlike knowledge. And yet here we find that *the love of Christ* surpasses real knowledge, and only then can we be full, complete. The curse of work finds its fulfillment not in riches or more work, but in the Christ of the New Testament.

As a teenager, I worked in a bank, handing out to eager children little cardboard kitty cats with slots inside for dimes. I, too, had saved dimes in the same way, until I realized I was truly dealing with small change. Now, trying to digest the passage in Ephesians, the truth makes me dizzy. Focusing on the wrong riches, we live an impoverished spiritual life while working ourselves into a frenzy to make ends meet. God waits to pour His riches—not His dimes, not His spare change—into my spiritual bank account, but I have zipped my heart tightly shut, like a puckered-mouthed old lady's closed pocketbook.

I'm using a child's penny saver, and God has a vault full of treasures for me. I'm living the life of a spiritual miser, hoarding my pathetic grubby resources, and this shows up in my relationships with my husband, children, friends, and neighbors. And the wealthiest Man in the universe is waiting to *hand* me—give me—all the spiritual wealth possible.

Imagine the richest man in the world standing around with unlimited free cash for anyone who will hold out a hand. Would we wait in line with our wheelbarrows or semis, or be skeptical and stay home?

And our God, who owns the cattle on a thousand hills, all the resources in the entire world, indeed, the world itself, asks us only to trust Him. To focus on Him and His provisions for us *one day a week*. To "deny ourselves and do no work." Yes, this is Old Testament law, but I think it's one of the most important things we can learn from the Law and its relationship to Eden's sweat-of-the-brow curse. And it is a bridge between Eden and Gethsemane where we meet Christ. While we still sweat it out in between the two gardens, Jesus approaches us from the other side, from the fulfillment.

Jesus and Gethsemane

Early in His ministry, Jesus drew fire from the religious ranks because He equated His work with the work of the Father. The listeners understood His meaning: He and the Father were one, equals. (They also wanted to kill Him for it.) But we find one of Jesus' most astounding assertions in John 17:4. He offered this prayer in the Upper Room, with His disciples present; Judas had just slipped away, a dark shadow, to rally the guards for the furtive arrest. "I glorified Thee on the earth, having accomplished the work which Thou hast given Me to do."

He had finished the work? How had Jesus possibly accomplished the work already? He hadn't been arrested, tried, crucified, done battle with the Evil One, risen from the dead, appeared to the disciples or to the others, or ascended to the Father. The world, in fact, was still a mess; the people were still under the rule of a foreign government; the disciples were mere hours away from abandoning all they'd been so lovingly taught.

Clearly, Jesus defined work differently than we do. To accomplish God's work does not mean we have finished everything on the world's to-do list. Jesus said, "This is the work of God, that you believe in Him whom He has sent" (John 6:29). This proves, indeed, to be work for us.

Though we still sweat and labor, Christ has labored for us. He accomplished the work God sent Him to do. Though painfully uncomfortable, we must go to the Garden, once again, to find the fulfillment of the work curse, the sweat of the brow curse.

In the Garden, in the thick darkness, Jesus agonized in private prayer, tormented over the coming sacrifice: " 'Father, if Thou art willing, remove this cup from Me; yet not My will, but Thine be done.' Now an angel from heaven appeared to Him, strengthening Him. And being in agony He was praying very fervently; and His sweat became like drops of blood, falling down upon the ground" (Luke 22:42–44).

No more need we earn our place, find our meaning by the sweat of our brow. We are connected to God irrevocably through the work of Christ in the Garden of Gethsemane, through the life of the risen Christ, who has accomplished the work God has given Him. This same Christ, who sweated great drops of blood that we might know Him and the power of His resurrection, now intercedes between us and the Father, ever working for us, enabling us to transform every waking, working moment into a sacrament, an offering of praise, to the glory of God.

⊠ *Listen*

. . . the mystery . . . has now been manifested to His saints, to whom God willed to make known what is the riches of the glory of this mystery . . . which is Christ in you, the hope of glory. And we proclaim Him, admonishing every man and teaching every man with all wisdom, that we may present every man complete in Christ. And for this purpose also I labor, striving according to His power, which mightily works within me. . . .

And whatever you do in word or deed, do all in the name of the Lord Jesus, giving thanks through Him to God the Father.

Colossians 1:26–29, 3:17

⊠ *Learn*

It may be difficult for the average Christian to get hold of the idea that his daily labors can be performed as acts of worship acceptable to God by Jesus Christ. . . . We must offer all our acts to God and believe that He accepts them. Then hold firmly to that position and keep insisting that every act of every hour of the day and night be included in the

*transaction. . . . Let us practice the fine art of making every work a
priestly ministration. Let us believe that God is in all our simple deeds
and learn to find Him there. . . . Let every man abide in the calling
wherein he is called and his work will be as sacred as the work of the
ministry. It is not what a man does that determines whether his work is
sacred or secular, it is* why *he does it. The motive is everything. Let a
man sanctify the Lord God in his heart and he can thereafter do no
common act.*

A. W. Tozer,
The Pursuit of God

🔀 *Live*

- ✦ When do you find yourself resenting your work, working harder than should be necessary to make ends meet?
- ✦ When have you experienced the Christ coming along beside you, inviting you to put your neck into His yoke, that He might share your burdens? (Matthew 11:28–30)
- ✦ When have you found your everyday work transformed into ministry for the glory of God?

23. BREAD IN THE GARDEN

Eden

Adam and Eve were amply provided for; they had food in abundance; but as a result of their sin, they would eat bread "by the sweat of their face." Before their "independence day," God both planted and grew the food to sustain them. The curse meant that they would be responsible now for their own bread, their own rations.

Because Adam and Eve were not content with the food God provided, hunger began to growl in all of us for God. We would try, will try, to fill that hunger with many things, including food, but we would also mistake that hunger for a desire for power, possessions, people. An insatiable craving for more would begin to characterize us, but the "more" can only be satisfied by God himself. Discontent would plague us, desires that could never be sated by material things. And our wandering eye—that term used for a person who cannot be faithful to one but always looks others over for possible appeasement—would lust after all sorts of bread. We would find it nearly impossible to be satisfied by our work, or the fruit of our labors. And because we were not content with the food God provided, we would be put in charge of the kitchens ourselves. (Perhaps this is why I dislike grocery shopping so much; it is part of the fall-out from the curse!)

Between Two Gardens

Between the gardens, the entire Jewish contingent packed their bags and girded up their loins for the great Exodus out of Egypt. God stopped His people and set up a ritual: Unleavened bread would be the staple to quicken their memories of how He passed over them to save them from the Egyptians. On the long march from slavery to the freedom of the Promised Land, God told the hungry and weary Israelites, "I will rain bread from heaven for you" (Exodus 16:4). And, because He knew their tendency—and ours—to store up for tomorrow out of fear, to overwork so we don't have to trust, God said, "It's a daily deal. You'll gather only enough for the day. Not for two days, or a week, or a year. Only on the day preceding the Sabbath will you gather enough for two days." And the people quickly found that if they collected the cowards' rations, the leftovers grew moldy and writhed with maggots. Could this be a grim picture of the soul that doesn't trust God, the God who provides?

This miracle food could only come from Yahweh. And as a reminder, when laying out the design of the tabernacle, and then the temple, God established the shewbread (or showbread) in the Holy Place. This "bread of the Presence" would always show others His graceful provision; in times of destitution and distress it would jog the memories of the Israelites about God's bread in the wilderness. Deeper within the tabernacle, in the Most Holy Place or Holy of Holies, a pot of manna resided, a souvenir (see Deuteronomy 8:3; Exodus 16:31–34; 25:16, 22, 30). In spite of Adam and Eve's quest for independence and control, God's huge love for us leads us to himself; He never intended for us to hunger without finding sustenance and nurture in, and through, Him.

Jesus

What amazes me is how God carries His people along—the bread in the wilderness, the offerings of bread, the pot of manna. Right out of the chute into ordained ministry, when Christ is whisked into the desert for tempting, He stands against Satan with the words, "Man shall not live on bread alone" (Matthew 4:4). Jesus lives it for us, showing us how to rely on Him and not on all the material things that woo us.

And is it any wonder that when the disciples said to Jesus, "Lord, teach us to pray," His words included, "Give us this day, our daily bread"? Again Christ prompts us, like the Alcoholics Anonymous phrase, "One day at a time." "Just trust me for this day; tomorrow has enough worries. Let's take today, friend," He says to us.

We watch Jesus take five loaves of barley bread and multiply them into food for thousands (John 6:9–13). Further on in John 6, Jesus urges His followers, "Do not work for the food which perishes, but for the food which endures to eternal life" (v. 27). The disciples want to cling to Moses and the miracle manna-in-the-wilderness story, but Jesus corrects them: "It is not Moses who has given you the bread out of heaven, but it is My Father who gives you the true bread out of heaven. For the bread of God is that which comes down out of heaven, and gives life to the world" (vv. 32–33).

And then, Jesus takes it a step further, proclaiming boldly, "I am the bread of life; he who comes to Me shall not hunger" (v. 35).

On the night before Christ's crucifixion, hours before His arrest in the Garden of Gethsemane, the Lord Jesus gathers those who have faithfully followed Him. They share the Passover meal together in a small room, commemorating God's faithful deliverance from slavery in Egypt. "And while they were eating, Jesus took some bread, and after a blessing, He broke it and gave it to the disciples, and said, 'Take, eat; this is My body'" (Matthew 26:26).

"And having taken some bread, when He had given thanks, He broke it, and gave it to them, saying, 'This is My body which is given for you; do this in remembrance of Me'" (Luke 22:19).

But the disciples don't remember.

After the wretched events of the crucifixion, numbed by grief and dismayed by their broken dreams, two of Jesus' followers drag wearily down the road to Emmaus. A man appears beside them, and they involve Him in their conversation as they rehash the events of

Golgotha and shake their heads in bewilderment. They walk together, two discouraged men and one whom they do not recognize. The stranger starts with Moses and begins to explain how it was necessary for the Christ to suffer these things. The day wears on. Nighttime crowds in and with it, undoubtedly, memories of darkness and horror. The two men say, "Stay with us. It's late." Luke 24:30 reads, "When He had reclined at the table with them, He took the bread and blessed it, and breaking it, He began giving it to them." In this act of taking the bread, blessing it, and offering the broken loaf to them, their eyes were opened. "He was recognized by them in the breaking of the bread" (Luke 24:35).

Even as baking bread creates a fragrance, luring us to the table, so the life of Christ and His words lure us to Him. His life becomes a fragrant aroma. Hunger for bread that endures, for eternal sustenance, growls within us until we acknowledge that only in Christ will we find our hunger satisfied. With the breaking of the Bread of Life, the curse of Eden—"by the sweat of your face you shall eat bread"—is broken forever.

🕸 *Listen*

I am the bread of life. Your fathers ate the manna in the wilderness, and they died. This is the bread which comes down out of heaven, so that one may eat of it and not die. I am the living bread that came down out of heaven; if any one eats of this bread, he shall live forever; and the bread also which I shall give for the life of the world is My flesh.

John 6:48–51

🕸 *Learn*

In Eden, Adam and Eve learned, "Eat and die." In Gethsemane, we learned, "Eat and live."

88 *Live*

- ✦ Of what does the scent of baking bread remind you?
- ✦ When, in brokenness, have you found Christ to be your sustenance?

24. THORNS IN THE GARDEN

For the gardener, for the human being, thorns and thistles are part of the package of tending the land. Adam and Eve's rebellion resulted in the curse of these hateful spined plants. After Eden, like dandelion fluff caught on the wind, thorns and thistles reproduce throughout the Old Testament, plaguing the Israelites in the form of enemies, scourging the land when the people left their plows and their God and followed the surrounding nations into captivity. But they are promised deliverance from the thorns and thistles, and the New Testament reveals the fulfillment.

Eden

While Adam and Eve shivered in their garments of leaves, God said of the ground they would tend, "Both thorns and thistles it shall grow for you." In their briarless world, Adam and Eve had no idea how wretched this curse would be. Like moving from a putting green to a carpet of cactus skin, shoes became mandatory apparel. They shed their barefoot innocence on exiting the first Garden.

Between Two Gardens

Growing up in southern Indiana, walking outside with bare feet meant thorns. We stepped lightly because of the locust trees, which bloomed beautifully white in spring and dropped outrageous quantities of thorns the rest of the year.

We reap the consequences of seeds sown in Eden: we tred gingerly to avoid puncture wounds; fruit comes with much more difficulty than thorns and thistles. In my own yard, those thistle plants shoot out runners instantly, in a hundred directions. If only we could devise a root system for helpful and productive plants! Some of my non-gardener friends share their tips on distinguishing weeds from flowers: If it comes up easily out of the ground when you pull on it, it's a good plant. The stuff with the complex, supportive root structure: that's a weed. And these complex roots, these runners, resemble the shooting out of sin in my life. Runners rip around underground, in the recesses of my heart, bearing thorns and thistles and barbs. If I miss the first deadly appearance, if I fail to jerk them out of my soul-soil instantly, they're off burrowing and sprouting and coming up everywhere in my spirit and my life.

Thorns and thistles pop up in the Old Testament, between the two gardens, as enemies. Ezekiel 28:24 speaks of a time when "there will be no more for the house of Israel a prickling brier or a painful thorn from any round about them who scorned them; then they will know that I am the Lord God." Joshua warned the Israelites, as he was preparing to die, that unfaithfulness on their part would result in the surrounding nations becoming "a whip on your sides and thorns in your eyes" (23:13).

And when hauled off into captivity for their unfaithfulness, the Israelites returned to a land thick with thorns and thistles and had to hack their way through the prickly, painful growth to once again plant and bear fruit. What a picture of the neglected, sin-and-thistle-ridden heart.

Hebrews 6:7–8 contrasts the porous soul that absorbs the rain and grows good fruit with the hard-souled person: "for ground that drinks the rain which often falls upon it and brings forth vegetation useful to those for whose sake it is also tilled, receives a blessing from God; but if it yields thorns and thistles, it is worthless and close to being cursed."

What mockery. We pretend to be royalty, pretend to have control of our lives, even as we fondle the thorny branches and plait them into a garland to wear around our hearts. Our gardens burst, but not with fruit. Rather, thorns and thistles choke the ground.

And Jesus, true royalty, the real King, endured the derision, wore the purple robe, and unflinchingly bore a taunting crown of thorns.

With Jesus, After the Garden of Gethsemane

The Scriptures tell us that the entire Roman cohort made a mockery of the assertion that Jesus was a king. They dressed Him up in a purple robe, wove a crown of thorns, and crushed it on His head. Shouting "Hail, King of the Jews!" they spit at him and alternately knelt and bowed before Him and beat Jesus' thorn-circled head with a reed.

But Christ ends this part of the curse when those who mocked and betrayed Him rammed a crown of thorns onto His brow. In one more instance of turning cursing into blessing, those thorns of mockery from the enemies actually signal the end of an era.

Isaiah prophesies of a time when "Instead of the thorn bush the cypress will come up; and instead of the nettle the myrtle will come up; and it will be a memorial to the Lord, for an everlasting sign which will not be cut off" (55:13). The thorns and thistles of Eden's curse would be no more, and their absence would be an eternal sign of the presence and power of God. By accepting that crown of thorns, and with His subsequent victory over sin and death, Christ has "put all His enemies under His feet" (1 Corinthians 15:25) and crushed the head of the Serpent.

Christ died with the thorns of our sin piercing His brow, blood from those thorns staining His face, running into His eyes.

I have a hard time with this. Especially in light of the thorns and thistles I allowed to grow up in my home, in my garden-heart, this week. Thorns of anger, of self-pity and self-absorption. Thistles that barricaded me off from loved ones, from God, from friends. I cordoned off my soul, and my joy, by allowing those cursed weeds to live here, take root, poison me. Amazingly, my thorns-and-thistles self does not alter Christ's work, His provision for the end of the curse.

How fascinating to realize that, in every curse, God moves between us and total realization of the effects of the curse. Providing bread—becoming bread; working by the sweat of our brow—fulfilling the work for us; cursing the land with thorns—wearing a mocking crown of thorns to signal their riddance. Never have we had to live totally without provision in the place of between; never have we fully been left to feel the entire ramifications of the curses. This is grace. This is Christ.

This is Gethsemane, and Golgotha, and a crown of thorns.

88 *Listen*

And they dressed Him up in purple, and after weaving a crown of thorns, they put it on Him; and they began to acclaim Him, "Hail, King of the

Jews!" And they kept beating His head with a reed, and spitting at Him, and kneeling and bowing before Him. And after they had mocked Him, they took the purple off Him, and put His garments on Him. And they led Him out to crucify Him.

Mark 15:17–20

❀ *Learn*

No more let sins and sorrows grow,
Nor thorns infest the ground;
He comes to make His blessings flow
Far as the curse is found,
Far as the curse is found,
Far as, far as the curse is found.

Isaac Watts,
"Joy to the World"

❀ *Live*

✦ Living with thorns and thistles becomes a choice. What hinders you in pulling out the barbs and prickly spines?

✦ With which sins are you most comfortable? How have you learned to work around them, catering to them, allowing them to infest the ground of your heart?

✦ What does the fulfillment of the curse of thorns and thistles mean for you?

$\mathcal{S}$even

FAILURE IN THE GARDEN

With hollowness filling my heart, I pulled the car out of my friend's driveway and began the long trip home. I had failed in a relationship very important to me, and during the drive back, other failures crowded into the car, leering and ugly, reminding me of my ineptitude in all areas. I quickly translated a failed friendship into a lifetime of failure.

For all of us, failure in some way is guaranteed. The absence of failure suggests perfection, a condition that ceased to exist after that fateful day in Eden.

Even our definition of failure fails, falls short, for failure in the world's eyes means failing to acquire the success, power, wealth, or status deemed appropriate and even necessary, the amount of which is usually determined by someone outside of ourselves. Thus every shortcoming represents not our humanity but our failure: the bounced check, the forgotten appointment, the messy house, the wayward child, the missed promotion or the demotion or job loss, the broken or hurting marriage. All these tempt us to classify ourselves as failures.

Perhaps, instead, they are marks of our inheritance, of our descent from Adam and Eve. They are signs, indeed, of our insufficiency and our imperfection.

In truth, failure fills the Scriptures: failed faith, failed morals, failed military campaigns, failed marriages, failed courage. Failed societies, failed systems, failed political reigns. Failure was rampant then, as it is now. Anything less than perfection qualifies, and we consistently score well below that mark. The learning curve is steep and slippery, and on it we are all novice skiers on Dead Man's Ridge.

Part of the stigma is that we see it from the world's eyes. Seen from the vantage point of eternity—the wide-angle lens—failure is necessary for redemption. Our failure puts us in the right place for God to triumph, for the saving life of Christ. Into the dark, dull void created by failure come the perfect life, faith, death, and resurrection of Jesus Christ.

25. FAILURE IN EDEN

Failure began during the infancy of creation, interrupting the perfect rhythm of a perfectly synchronized world. It began with a story less familiar to us: the story of an angel, fallen from heaven, taking the form of a serpent (see Isaiah 14:12–20). The failure quickly contaminated God's most precious creations: Adam and Eve.

Adam and Eve's failure, perhaps above all else, was a failure to trust God: God's goodness, God's promise, God's provisions. When they averted their eyes from God and toward themselves, when they ceased to listen to His Word and began to weigh truth on a different scale, their focus became what they had not rather than what they had.

Anytime we swivel our gaze away from God toward ourselves and the outspoken tauntings and temptings of another—in this case, Satan dressed in snakeskin—we are in danger. Whether we compare tangible goods or intangibles, comparison seldom leads to contentment, is rarely a positive tool, and sets us up for failure.

Adam and Eve failed when they began to trust their own abilities, to seek a wisdom and a measuring scale other than God's. We imitate our predecessors with nearly every breath.

Current marketing savvy tells us that failure is deliberate. This focus on failure led *Time Magazine* to vote Jeff Bezos, founder of amazon.com, the on-line bookseller, "Person of the Year," even though his company lost a reported $350 million in 1999. While business may say, "Failure is part of the plan," this sounds remarkably like a child falling off a bike, dabbing off the blood, and saying, "I meant to do that." Rationalization is a remarkable tool! Can we truly say that failure is a badge of honor? Failure is no honor, just as the failure of Adam and Eve in the Garden elicited no merits, no commendations, no award for trying. How, exactly, is failure part of the plan, and is it truly helpful in today's society?

Interpreting Failure

Avoiding failure is like avoiding stepping on cracks on a mosaic-tiled floor; however, it is not always consoling to remember that failure means we are alive. If failure is part and parcel of living in this world, regardless of whether we compare ourselves to others or simply go about our lives from day to day, how we deal with failure becomes crucial.

Our friends in Eden chose to hide behind leaves to cover up their failure. Their second reaction was blame. Failure became an opportunity to cast about, laying the cause at another's feet. This technique carries many people through their entire lives, as they justify their own shortcomings and failures by pointing to poor or inadequate treatment from others. By blame, however, we defer not only responsibility, but also growth. As Father John Powell said, "Growth begins where blaming ends."[1]

Like driving a stake into mud or hammering a nail into soft wood, failure too easily allows us to pound ourselves down, endlessly rehashing details, spiraling, infecting mood and thought, working our failure like worry beads. Every additional failure or mistake, however tiny, feeds into the pond of despair, confirming, like an endless echo in a canyon, our worthlessness.

Did an inability to let go of their failure haunt Adam and Eve for the rest of their lives? Did they replay the tape to one another in the dark of night, saying, "If only . . ."? When did they cease to blame each other for their own failure and come fully into God's presence, owning their past and turning it over to their Creator and Redeemer? I'm learning that the shorter the time between failure, blame, ownership, and relinquishment, the quicker I enter into a place of grace, where God can redeem my failures.

Interpreting another's failure toward us is different, however. Here we must begin to understand our own take on another's failure. Do they, for instance, fail us because *we* are somehow worthy of better treatment? Do we assume another's failure as rejection, indicative of our state or status? Do we feel shock, anger, surprise, disappointment? Perhaps. And these feelings vary wildly; the more we are separated from our own fallenness and failings, the more we are disconnected from the truth about ourselves.

Perhaps, though, our reaction is one of denial. We need the illusion of another's perfection and refuse to believe a report of a loved one's infidelity, or another's dishonesty or harmful behavior. We refuse the truth: We are all broken, incomplete, and prone to falls and to stumbling and to flat-out failures.

When a loved one fails, we translate this as a reflection on our own image, our own worth; we slide into this like a custom-made shoe. A child's trouble at school creates unease and feelings of failure in us as parents. A spouse's failure makes us look bad. When we cannot separate our feelings about ourselves from another's behavior, a sense of failure looms. Internalizing another's failure as our own becomes a dangerous pastime, because failure is global.

No one is exempt. (Nor is it particularly our job to tell others how far they fall from the perfect ten!)

So what is our ideal reaction to failure? Feeding on failure—our own or another's, corporate failure or societal failure—is equivalent to drinking weed killer. Failure has a purpose just as weed killer does, but if misused it can be deadly.

🔀 *Listen*

Though the fig tree should not blossom,
And there be no fruit on the vines,
Though the yield of the olive should fail,
And the fields produce no food,
Though the flock should be cut off from the fold,
And there be no cattle in the stalls,
Yet I will exult in the Lord,
I will rejoice in the God of my salvation.
The Lord God is my strength,

And He has made my feet like hinds' feet,
And makes me walk on my high places.

Habakkuk 3:17–19

❈ *Learn*

The mark of a broken leader is that he or she has a much deeper gratitude for the mercy and grace of our Lord. Unless we have wrestled with God in our own disappointment and come out limping, we are not broken. And it is only through authentic brokenness that we will be able to channel God's mercy and grace to our colleagues, coworkers, and congregations when they disappoint us or let us down. In our own unbroken strength, we are more apt to "wash our hands" of people we deem unfit or who don't measure up to their calling. This hardness of heart leads to disaster in ministry. We must unmask our own stubborn self-will and deal with it. Genuine brokenness is the only posture that prepares us adequately for the spiritual battles we face.

Joseph L. Umidi,
Confirming the Pastoral Call

❈ *Live*

◆ When have you internalized another's failure as your own? With whom, and when, are you most vulnerable to this transference?

◆ What is your typical reaction to failure?

◆ How do you give it over to God?

26. Failure Between Two Gardens

Americans cut their teeth on competition: first steps (my baby walked sooner than yours did!), first grades, first team, first boyfriend or girlfriend, first job . . . We want to be on the first-place team, take first place in any ranking, and we pass that gift on to our children. Here, no one sews badges on their vest for failure. The red ribbon always means almost, and bronze is never gold. Failure is comparison-based and performance-based, and disqualifies us instantly from first place. In America, as a T-shirt reminds us, "Second place is the first loser."

Pictures are scattered along shelves in Andrew's parents' den. Six boys of varying ages peer out from the frames. Their father held strong ideas about competition, teamwork, and their tie-in with worth. The boys in front, dressed in their baseball uniforms, hold championship trophies. The boys in back, also in uniform, each hold up a sign that reads, "Loser."

Does anyone really believe "it's how you play the game"?

Faces of Failure

Failure trails Adam and Eve out of Eden, filling the Scriptures. The interesting part of failure, however, is that failure marked a change for many of our friends in the Old Testament. Abram got a new name after failure, becoming Abraham (Genesis 17:5). Jacob used God's new name for him, Israel, after his beloved wife Rachel died (Genesis 35:16–20). Israel means, "he fights or persists with

God." David's moral failure with Bathsheba, and his faithful processing of that failure, ultimately led to a son who would lead Israel, and from whom would come the Messiah. The list continues. Moses never entered the Promised Land, Sarah laughed in the face of God's promise to have a child, Elijah sunk so low he could not get up from his despondency. Shifting to the New Testament, a little research uncovers the fact that most of the disciples were dropouts, rejects from theological school! These "failures" were the people with whom Jesus would entrust the most vital message of all time!

Thankfully, performance has nothing to do with the love of God for His people. In fact, looking at the Scriptures, *unfailing* is one of God's attributes.

Unfailing

The failures of the people do indeed riddle the Scriptures. Three truths, however, stand out, flying in the face of failure-prone living:

- ✦ *God does not fail.* Zephaniah 3:5 reads, "The Lord is righteous. . . . He will do no injustice. Every morning He brings His justice to light; He does not fail."

- ✦ *God's Word has not failed.* In Joshua 23:14, Joshua reminds the Israelites and us, "You know in all your hearts and in all your souls that not one word of all the good words which the Lord your God spoke concerning you has failed; all have been fulfilled for you, not one of them has failed."

- ✦ *Love never fails.* The "love chapter," 1 Corinthians 13, lauds the attributes of love, not the least of which is found in verse 8: "Love never fails."

If, then, one of God's characteristics is unfailing love; if we are reminded continuously of God's faithfulness; then failure this side of heaven must bring about some redemption. Failure, as a tool, somehow brings us to a place of whole-hearted (or *wholer*-hearted) trust. It then becomes part of the plan.

However, though we live in the "age of instant," instantly moving from failure's darkness into the brilliant daylight of lessons learned does not give us bouquets of praise. I've tried this with plants, sheltered in a house all winter long—taken them into full sunlight unfiltered by glass and walls and roof. First they sunburn, then they turn into bagel chips. I destroy a winter's worth of careful tending in one day.

One of the problems with Christianity is that we leap too quickly from tragedy or trial to "Hallelujah! All is a blessing." If we faithfully process the pain of failure and our own human nature, somewhere in between, like the darkness between stark Friday and Easter Sunday, is a place of absolute loss: a place where we can say, with Job, "I brought nothing into the world, will take nothing out." This middle ground, cratered with doubt and shrouded with the clouds of reckoning, brings us, finally, to the end of ourselves. A place of utter reliance on, and gratitude toward, the God who never fails. Only then can we honestly finish Job's statement, "Blessed be the name of the Lord" (Job 1:21).

Failure is only successful (if we must use that term) if it brings us closer to the sufficiency of God. In failure, we learn to rely not on our own abilities, but on the ability of God to bring about redemption of even the worst failure.

🏵 *Listen*

Something crazy has happened, for it's obvious that you no longer have the crucified Jesus in clear focus in your lives. His sacrifice on the Cross was certainly set before you clearly enough. Let me put this question to you: How did your new life begin? Was it by working your heads off to please God? Or was it by responding to God's Message to you? . . . Only crazy people would think they could complete by their own efforts what was begun by God. If you weren't smart enough or strong enough to begin it, how do you suppose you could perfect it? Did you go through this whole painful learning process for nothing? . . .

Answer this question: Does the God who lavishly provides you with his own presence, his Holy Spirit, working things in your lives you could never do for yourselves, does he do these things because of your strenuous moral striving or because you trust him to do them in you?

. . . anyone who tries to live by his own effort, independent of God, is doomed to failure. Scripture backs this up: "Utterly cursed is every person who fails to carry out every detail written in the Book of the law."

Selections from Galatians 3
The Message

⌘ *Learn*

God, of your goodness give me yourself; for you are sufficient for me. I cannot properly ask anything less, to be worthy of you. If I were to ask less, I should always be in want. In you alone do I have all.

Juliana of Norwich, England,
15th Century

So, what do we do with sin? What is the humble response to our inevitable failure? Sin surely offends the heart of a holy God, so we never want to take it lightly. How are we to ensure that it is dealt with, yet not give in to an unhealthy obsession with our own shortcomings? We must remember that we are spiritual beings who, for now, battle this body of flesh. We will sin. If we deny it, we are deceived; if we ignore it, we risk grieving the Holy Spirit (1 John 1:8; Ephesians 4:22).

Instead of trying to stir up a sense of sinfulness, we call upon God's Spirit to do His work. While we invite conviction on the basis of His righteousness, we cry out at the same time for restoration on the basis of His mercy. If we don't do this, we will end up being endlessly self-absorbed, counteracting the very work God seeks to do in our hearts. All sin, though grievous to our souls, should only serve to catapult us to His side, ravenous for a touch of grace.

Tricia McCary Rhodes,
Taking Up Your Cross

88 *Live*

✦ What is your most humbling "failure"? How do you separate your sense of self from events of failure?
✦ What have you learned about yourself in times of failure? About others? About your faith?
✦ Where have you experienced God in the midst of failure?

27. FAILURE IN GETHSEMANE

How can it be that our very faith hinges on the life, death, and accomplishments of One whom the world determined a failure? Jesus, it seems, was a total failure: He failed in the eyes of everyone who knew Him. Socially, politically, culturally, and religiously, Jesus failed. He did not marry, did not have a home or a decent-paying job (all symbols of success), and wandered around like a transient. Christ lived a countercultural life, inverting all the norms of popular living, calling the meek blessed and the poor rich and the persecuted fortunate.

Jesus failed to deliver Israel from political occupation; failed to convince even His disciples—His closest friends—of His plan and purpose. He didn't ride into the city on a white horse, He perched on an unbroken donkey. His life was immediately exchanged for the life and freedom of a known criminal, Barabbas, and He died the death of a lowlife, hanging naked on a cross in full view of a mocking, spitting, hate-filled crowd.

I don't think, frankly, that the disciples shouted T.G.I.F. as the guards battered their Lord and shattered their dreams. I don't think even God would call that Friday "good." Not from the world's eyes, using the system's measure of success. Nor did the disillusioned disciples holler "Thank God for failure" as they watched all their hopes and plans die on a cross, the ultimate symbol of failure.

But God has never measured success or failure using the world's superficial standards. First Corinthians 1:27–29 tells us, "But God chose the foolish things of the world to shame the wise; and God chose the weak things of the world to shame the strong. He chose the lowly things of this world and the despised things—and the things that are not—to nullify the things that are, so that *no one may boast before Him*" (NIV, emphasis added).

If we're going to rely on superficiality, then Christ is a stumbling block. A failure. But if we are going to rely on God, then the cross of Christ, the life and death and resurrection of the Lord Jesus, stand like a lighthouse in the dismal darkness of all our failure and redeem us. Ironically, into the failure that is death, death that began in Eden and should never have happened, God brings about fulfillment. Christ revolutionizes our idea of failure and redefines our notions of success. And He reminds us, who are constantly falling into the potholes of failure and wrenching emotional and spiritual ankles, that our brokenness, our weakness, even our failures, become opportunities to be shaped and molded into the likeness of Jesus. In our failures God can be glorified, when we turn them into opportunities for trust, for growth, and for new life.

Sifting

In the intimacy of the Upper Room, with a donkey tethered outside, Jesus demonstrated to His followers the life of a servant by washing their feet, and He instituted what we now call the Lord's Supper. In this place of closeness and teaching, Jesus turned to Peter and said, "Simon, Simon, behold, Satan has demanded permission to sift you like wheat; but I have prayed for you, that your faith may not fail; and you, when once you have turned again, strengthen your brothers" (Luke 22:31–32).

Peter responded instantly with denial: "Lord, with You I am ready to go both to prison and to death!" (v. 33). But Jesus knew better, knew that before the rooster crowed three rounds, Peter would deny ever knowing Him. Jesus knew that Peter would embrace the bitterest of failure and disillusionment, and Jesus also understood that failure would not be fatal, but would rather become a tool to strengthen others.

We, too, have brashly asserted our faithfulness, only to hear the mocking call of the cock, ridiculing our best efforts and reminding us not of our faith, but of our failure. And we, too, have the same choice available to us that was available to Peter: once we have turned, we strengthen others.

Every time Elizabeth looked at her wedding ring, she heard that rooster. She remembered her vow to love, cherish, and remain faithful to her husband; remembered the horrid stumbling, the affair she'd never intended to have, the relationship that promised heaven and delivered hell, and the bitter agony of moral failure. Remembered, too, her husband's love for her and his choosing her, again, and their choice, together, to rebuild their marriage in spite of her failure. And her choice, now, to guide others on those dangerous coastlines away from the treacherous rocks of adultery, by helping them understand the signs leading toward unfaithfulness and helping to build, rather than to destroy, their marriages. Like Peter, Elizabeth had a choice: to lose herself in her failure, to destroy her family and marriage and faith; or to turn back toward God and honesty and healing, and having turned, to help others.

Following Peter's failure is an amazing moment, a life-changing, world-changing interaction. The Scriptures tell us (Luke 22:54–62) that after the third person says, "Certainly this man also was with Him, for he is a Galilean too," Peter answers harshly, "Man, I do not know what you are talking about." The cock crows the third time before the last word has even died on Peter's tongue.

It takes my breath away. The very next verse says, "And the Lord turned and looked at Peter."

Imagine the place of your greatest failure. Freeze the frame: feel the blackness, the hollow ugliness, the crushing disappointment, the self-hatred. Stay there. And then, in the courtyard of your failure, watch Jesus. Watch the Man you love, the One you have vowed to follow until death itself. Even as He is heading into a place of torture and crucifixion, He turns. And meets your eyes.

And offers you love.

And you turn, and strengthen others.

This, friend, is redemption. This is failure turned to glory for the sake of Jesus.

🟎 *Listen*

And [the Lord] has said to me, "My grace is sufficient for you, for power is perfected in weakness." Most gladly, therefore, I will rather boast about my weaknesses, that the power of Christ may dwell in me. Therefore, I am well content with weaknesses, with insults, with distresses, with persecutions, with difficulties, for Christ's sake; for when I am weak, then I am strong.

2 Corinthians 12:9–10

🟎 *Learn*

"It is God's choosing of us as His children that counts, not our betrayal of that choice. Hidden deeply in our actions of betrayal and faithlessness is the heart of a child, where a calling to be a child of God can still be heard. This capacity cannot be destroyed, either through failure or through self-inflicted death. For death does not have that power; it cannot kill what God has made alive. And what we have killed within ourselves, God can and will make alive through the life of His Son, Jesus Christ."

Ray S. Anderson,
The Gospel According to Judas

🟎 *Live*

◆ When have you stood in the courtyard of failure? Describe your feelings.

✦ Can you imagine yourself in Peter's place, meeting the Lord's eyes? What do you read in His gaze?

✦ Write a letter to God, describing your feelings of failure and your experience of His presence.

Eight

EXILE AND THE GARDEN

For the final two years of his life [Dietrich] Bonhoeffer was a prisoner of the Third Reich, confined for the first eighteen months to . . . a cell room, six by nine feet, characterized by the simplest and humblest accommodation—a hard, narrow bed, a shelf, a stool, a bucket and a skylight window. This scarcely promised to be a setting in which some of the most creative theological thinking of the twentieth century could be born. It did, however, become precisely that as the months of confinement passed."[1]

Thoughts of exile remind us of prisoners, of those suffering unjustly because of "crimes against the government," but who are in actuality, or ultimately, imprisoned for their faith. Transferred from prison to prison, Dietrich Bonhoeffer bore witness of the joy of knowing and following Christ. He penned numerous letters as he lived out his faith within those walls, letters that were smuggled out by a sympathetic guard and eventually published as *Letters and Papers from Prison* (Macmillan, 1972). In one letter, Bonhoeffer writes,

I am so sure of God's guiding hand that I hope I shall always be kept in that certainty. You must never doubt that I'm travel-ing with gratitude and cheerfulness along the road where I'm being led. My past life is brim-full of God's goodness, and my sins are covered by the forgiving love of Christ crucified.[2]

Without the aid of others' writing and films, most of us cannot imagine the horror of exile, nor the challenge exile represents to the spirit. Exile, we do know, always casts another in the role of judge; and yet, exile need not be crippling to the soul and may actually be a means of great grace, as history demonstrates. We begin in the first Garden, with Adam and Eve's grasping after control and god-like power, then travel through the Old Testament and into our own lives. We will move with Christ, as He was exiled outside the City of David, into the final Garden, which ultimately has power to transform our own exile, our own alienation and separation from God.

28. Adam and Eve and the Garden Exile

No longer innocent, after not only reaching for and eating the ripe, lovely forbidden fruit, but after covering up their sin and hid-ing from God, Adam and Eve were in danger of living in permanent separation from their Creator. When they exiled God from their hearts, God, as an act of great grace and mercy, drove them—the word means thrust, hurled, expelled—from the Garden of Eden. Though God had not withheld the fruit of the Tree of Life, now, lest they eat from that tree and live forever in their state of death,

He cast them out. It sounds rough, harsh, and judgmental, but this would be their salvation.

Their physical exile became a tangible reminder of their spiritual self-exile—forever they would remember Eden. Certain scents would pull them back to that place of perfection and to the cause of their exile.

Adam and Eve also saw in the very next act of creation—their physical union and the birth of their first two children—the outworking of their exile. The consequences for choosing to live in separation from God meant that their own children would suffer. The first Adam would go down in history as the one who exiled an entire world from God and set in motion a life of seeking, of wandering.

Though undoubtedly they heard nostalgic stories of the first Garden, Cain and Abel would never know paradise. But they would know jealousy, and coveting, and revenge, and the logical conclusion to these, when unrestrained: murder. Not unlike his parents, longing for what seemed better, reaching for what did not belong to him, Cain envied Abel his offering. Perhaps, too, Cain coveted Abel's relationship with God, his heart that sought after God. But the power to give life and to take life away belongs only to God, and in taking his brother's life, murdering him in the field, Cain, like his parents before him, sought to become like God.

And thus the exile would continue.

88 *Listen*

The Lord builds up Jerusalem;
He gathers the outcasts of Israel.
He heals the brokenhearted,
And binds up their wounds.

Psalm 147:2–3

88 *Learn*

We live in our world as people in exile, forever wandering, moving, separating from family and friends. Is there, beneath this permanent nomadic lifestyle, a longing for home, for the original place of safety? And, in our state of constant seeking, are we becoming like Cain, taking the power of life in our hands, coveting the next better job, home, car, income? And if so, if we become like Cain, who is Abel?

Jane Rubietta

88 *Live*

✦ What are the ramifications of exile in your own life? From childhood through adult years, when have you felt outcast, expelled?

✦ How does exile impact your relationships with loved ones? With your God? With yourself?

29. IN EXILE: BETWEEN THE GARDENS

Exile from Eden set the pattern for a life of wandering exile. God told Adam and Eve's firstborn son, Cain, "You shall be a vagrant and a wanderer on the earth." Cain reacted immediately, whining and protesting, even though he'd murdered his only brother: "My punishment is too great to bear! Behold, Thou hast driven me this day from the face of the ground; and from Thy face I shall be hidden, and I shall be a vagrant and a wanderer on the earth, and it will come about that whoever finds me will kill me!" (Genesis 4:12–14).

Even as Adam and Eve hid from God, so Cain's words, "From Thy face I shall be hidden," echo the horrid consequence of separation from God. This tears at my parent-heart, a heart that desires the very best for my children, and must have broken God's heart. But God, full of mercy, did not leave Cain helpless or unprotected. He appointed a sign, or mark, designating him as untouchable by enemies and ever reminding Cain of his Creator's gracious love and protection.

He does the same for us today. He marks us as His own, sealing us with the Holy Spirit of promise for our protection. He has not given Satan, the Serpent, power over our souls. Through Christ, God promises us, "No temptation has overtaken you but such as is common to man; and God is faithful, who will not allow you to be tempted beyond what you are able, but with the temptation will provide the way of escape also, that you may be able to endure it" (1 Corinthians 10:13). Undertones of temptation haunted the story of Cain, but Cain refused to listen to the truth, the possibility of mastering sin. Before Cain killed his brother, God had told him, "If you do well, will not your countenance be lifted up? And if you do not do well, sin is crouching at the door; and its desire is for you, but you must master it" (Genesis 4:7).

Cain, apparently true to his destiny, finally settled in the land called Nod, which—no surprise!—means "wandering, exile" (Genesis 4:16). Every day of his life he would be reminded of his choice, marked by the decision to take life rather than to honor it.

Exile the Enemy

The word for "driven" in Genesis 4:14 is the same as is used of God's driving Cain's parents out of Eden: Adam and Eve's son was also thrust out, expelled from the family farm. This word is again used to describe God's action in the lives of the Israelites, when He promised to "drive out" the enemies from before them. He vowed to expel the Hivite, the Canaanite, and the Amorite from the Promised Land. The Israelites, however, figured they could strike a bargain with some of those enemies and let the enemies live among them.

God is quite willing to go before us, as He was with the Israelites, to drive out the enemies and to clear a path for us. Our response sounds strikingly like the Israelites', our choice like Cain's; we are not much different today. We choose exile and alienation when we allow enemies to camp in our garden, to pitch their tents in our soul's soil. The stakes often are pushed deeply into our lives— whether emotions gone awry like anger turned to rage, or coveting or fear, which lead us either to build up treasures on the earth or to hide.

We are comfortable with our enemies, fraternizing and making treaties with them. "I'll cover for you. You can stay as long as you don't show your face to anyone else." Or our enemies pretend a friendship, and bargain with us, "I'll let you keep living as long as you keep our relationship—this sin—between us." Like violence, pornography, living a two-level lifestyle (pious at church on Sunday, a horror in the home), the closet drinker, the person with an addiction to painkillers, the romance addict—these are secret relationships that we allow to live, like mold in a damp basement, in the hidden places of our hearts.

God would drive them out, exile them, but instead, we choose to live in a personal exile, for the split life is a life of exile from God.

Exile the Unclean

Hundreds of verses in the Old Testament warn about uncleanness. God is holy, and uncleanness separates God's people from Him. The seemingly rigorous fastidiousness—about eating the right food, not touching "unclean" people or animals or substances, not engaging in unclean acts—was about relationship. God, who is holy, could not walk about their camp with its uncleanness. Uncleanness separates us from God, exiles us, and God wants to be part of our lives.

No uncleanness was allowed in the camp, or in the Holy City, or in the temple or tabernacle. For instance, because a dead body was considered unclean, elaborate arrangements were made in the event of a priest dying in the Most Holy Place. If the bells on the ends of the priest's garments stopped jingling, the priest attending outside the doorway would tug on the pull rope, to drag the dead body outside the holy place. Death was not to be part of the City of Life or the Holy of Holies, just as it was not intended to be part of Eden.

In light of further admonitions against uncleanness, the Israelites carried waste outside the camp, and outside the city when Jerusalem was built, where they disposed of it. Those with infectious diseases were to cry out, "Unclean! Unclean!" if someone passed by, thus signaling that no one could touch them. The Scriptures tell us that "As long as he has the infection he remains unclean. He must live alone; he must live outside the camp" (Leviticus 13:46 NIV).

How often, I wonder, do we exile another after judging him or her unclean? We exile others emotionally, alienating them when they do something less than perfect, or different than we expect, or if they treat us as somehow less than we deserve. Perhaps they dress inappropriately or don't look good enough to be with us, or their mannerisms are embarrassing, so we exclude them. Forgetting an important date or event is grounds for a freeze-out. We send them outside the camp, becoming like God to avenge our hurt (which is often the underground root of anger and judgment).

Or we exile ourselves, pulling away in self-judgment, pushing others off. Unclean! Stay away from me! We become emotional lepers, living in the outhouse instead of letting Christ carry our shame, anger, hurt.

We exile our children when they aren't perfect, looking at them sternly over our judge's half-glasses. Our neighbor, the pastor, a co-worker, the cashier—no one is exempt from our perfection-seeking, judgment-rendering exile.

Useful Exile

Exile can be transforming, however. Typically, when the Israelites were exiled for their sinful ways, their idolatry, God's intent was that exile move them to repentance and change. In this way exile becomes a type of spiritual formation, a place where our losses and alienation wean us from dependency on all, save God.

Hezekiah's son, King Manasseh, was so evil that blood ran in the streets of Jerusalem (2 Kings 21:16), so evil that God removed him from the throne and exiled him to Assyria, a country renowned for its torturous treatment of prisoners. Exile transformed him, breaking his idolatrous heart and leading him back to God. Lynn Austin, in book five of her historical fiction series "Chronicles of the King,"[3] describes his anger and then desperation while in exile, a desperation descending into near madness, until the king's face-off with his sin. As God showed him the wickedness in his heart, Manasseh found relief only in the loving presence and undeserved forgiveness of his heavenly Father. We know this because of the changes he instituted after returning from exile. This challenges us in our own exile to continue to transform the world because of our own transformation. Second Chronicles 33:15–16 tells us, "[Manasseh] got rid of the foreign gods and removed the image from the temple of the Lord, as well as all the altars he had built on the temple hill and in Jerusalem; and he threw them out of the city. Then he restored the altar of the Lord and sacrificed fellowship offerings and thank offerings on it, and told Judah to serve the Lord, the God of Israel" (NIV).

While in exile, we have a choice. The best choice, of course, is to turn to God and allow His grace to heal and transform our exile, helping us to bloom in the desert, making true the Scripture, "Their life shall be like a watered garden" (Jeremiah 31:12).

⊠ *Listen*

When they are in the land of their enemies, I will not reject them, nor will I so abhor them as to destroy them, breaking My covenant with them; for I am the Lord their God. But I will remember for them the covenant with their ancestors, whom I brought out of the land of Egypt in the sight of the nations, that I might be their God. I am the Lord.

Leviticus 26:44–45

⊠ *Learn*

[Many] well-known dissidents from Russia and other repressive regimes . . . had a tremendous influence on the church and even society at large while they were in prison. But what happened to them once they were released? Aleksandr Solzhenitsyn moved to America, became a millionaire, made a couple of good speeches while the people were still

listening, and then lost his influence. I'm glad that he has now returned to Russia, but I fear his opportunity to make a real difference there may have passed.

Brother Andrew,
For the Love of My Brothers

88 *Live*

+ What enemies do you allow to live in your garden?
+ What promises of God can comfort and encourage you? How can you relinquish them to God, that He might exile, drive them out?
+ Might this be a time of exile, either self- or other-imposed? How might God desire to transform you during this season?

30. THE FINAL EXILE:
"OUTSIDE THE CAMP"

The pictures portraying Jesus as weak and emaciated fascinate and confound me. After reading and rereading the Gospels, the steel-like strength of His faith and character, and His endless love, leave me wordless. Never in history has a man of such determination lived. Jesus, our Jesus, was no foreigner to exile. An angel warned Joseph in a dream that Herod was searching for their newborn Son and said, "Arise and take the Child and His mother, and flee to Egypt" (Matthew 2:13). His parents took Him and escaped by night to Egypt, where they stayed until Herod's death.

In another dream, an angel appeared to Joseph and instructed him to take the family and go back to Israel. But back in their homeland, Joseph learned that Herod's son reigned over Jerusalem, and he was afraid to go there. God warned him in a dream to flee again, to Galilee.

And then, after years of apprenticeship with His father, Jesus' very ministry was inaugurated by exile. A similar word for "drove out" from the Old Testament is used for Jesus' being driven out, thrust out, hurled into the wilderness (Mark 1:12).

Jesus knew life on the run; exile was woven into the very fabric of His experience. Echoing the strains of Eden's departure, we hear His words to a scribe, "The foxes have holes, and the birds of the air have nests; but the Son of Man has nowhere to lay His head" (Matthew 8:20).

An outcast himself, Jesus feared no reprisal from touching a fellow outcast. When a leper came to Him, bowed down to Him, saying, "Lord, if You are willing, You can make me clean," this Son of Man did not scream, "Unclean! Unclean!" No. Christ stretched out His hand and touched him, saying, "I am willing; be cleansed" (Matthew 8:2–3).

Jesus also drove out, cast out, ejected, thrust away, the vendors who wanted to pollute the temple and distract the worshipers and pervert their relationship with God. "You cannot buy that restoration, that forgiveness, with God, nor the proper sacrifice," He seemed to say. Christ alone could purchase that relationship, securing it for all eternity.

But while Adam and Eve were exiled *from* the Garden of Eden, Christ was ultimately exiled *to* the Garden, to Gethsemane, where enemies arrested Him and led Him away to the Place of the Skull.

Christ was crucified "outside the camp," exiled from the Holy

City, the City of David, the place where His followers hoped He would reign. Christ was cast out by friends, rulers, religious people, and ultimately God. Christ, the Second Adam (see 1 Corinthians 15:45) also had to be exiled, driven out of the camp, that He might conquer all the enemies. "For [Christ] must reign until He has put all His enemies under His feet" (1 Corinthians 15:25).

That Jesus *chose* exile, voluntarily going outside the camp, stuns me. I cannot understand such love or such overwhelming—what? Integrity? Strength? I am well aware that going into exile with Christ, meeting Him outside the camp, sharing His disgrace, requires application. I cannot go into exile with Christ and not be changed by that exile.

May God help us to be willing to change, to be transformed as a result of meeting Christ in exile. For Christ suffered, outside the city gate, bearing our reproach, our uncleanness, that we might never again know alienation and exile from God. Though the exile's mirror shows an emaciated, skeletal face—the face of the living dead—the mirror of the soul reflects good health, a joy undaunted by starvation and deprivation, a heart fed and filled by the continual presence and comfort of God in Christ Jesus.

88 *Listen*

The high priest carries the blood of animals into the Most Holy Place as a sin offering, but the bodies are burned outside the camp. And so Jesus also suffered outside the city gate to make the people holy through his own blood. Let us, then, go to him outside the camp, bearing the disgrace he bore. For here we do not have an enduring city, but we are looking for the city that is to come.

Hebrews 13:11–14 NIV

🞬 *Learn*

The people who love . . . are the most revolutionary people on earth. They are the ones who upset all values; they are the explosives in human society. [But they are also those] whom they want to get rid of, whom they declare an outlaw, whom they kill.

Dietrich Bonhoeffer,
from a sermon

🞬 *Live*

✦ How are we called to bear Christ's disgrace "outside the camp"? When, for instance, have you experienced the disgrace of exile?

✦ What does it mean to you, to be transformed by meeting Christ in exile?

Nine

SUFFERING IN THE GARDEN

Rain slashed against the blank windowpanes like needles hitting metal. The darkness and gloom outside mimicked the darkness inside my soul. In the hospital waiting room, I wrestled with the intense physical and emotional pain loved ones were experiencing. Their suffering burned a hole in my heart like acid. I had to be careful not to close my eyes. In the dark, the tears rushed to the sealed shutters and pressed their way through, bullies with a shoulder push.

The next day, my son and I walked to the playroom on the children's floor of the hospital. We both stopped to admire a toddler in a yellow T-shirt that reached nearly to the floor. She wore matching fuzzy yellow footies that practically glowed against the floor's linoleum, and her beaming smile charmed and warmed our cold, tired, and frightened hearts.

Only on the way back to the room did I see the five-inch scar wrapping over the baby's head and down the side of her scalp.

So much pain. My own is only a microcosm; the pain I feel for others is a drop in the huge ocean of suffering in this world. Since the seed of suffering was planted in Eden ("I will greatly increase your pains in childbearing; with pain you will give birth to children . . . through painful toil . . ." Genesis 3:16–17 NIV), its roots have wrapped around the lives of individuals. We live in a world where pain isn't an elective course, like Ballroom Dancing. Suffering seems to be a curriculum requirement to get our degree, and it's both a by-product of our faith and a by-product of garden choices.

31. Rooted in Eden

As suffering works through the soil of our lives, it assumes different forms. The "Voice of the Martyrs" Web site (*www.vom.org*) estimates that two hundred million Christians are currently persecuted for their faith.[1] But at this time in history, few of us in the Western world experience actual persecution for our Christianity, at least not the outright torture and oppression of many far-away relatives in the body of Christ.

In Saudi Arabia, for instance, a convert to Christianity can expect estrangement, deportation, or even death at the hands of family members. In Sudan, faith in Christ means slavery and genocide.[2]

Many experience less dramatic but still real consequences for their faith when friends or family members or even associates at church see them take a stand for integrity or holiness, and mock or ostracize them. When Mark refused to gossip about the pastor with other church staff, they excluded him, undermining his ministry and his reputation. (The jokes and rib-poking experienced because of weird hair or out-of-style clothing or just plain antisocial "religious" behavior are not included in the suffering-for-your-faith category.)

Whether or not we are persecuted outright for belief in Christ, other types of suffering are valid, sprouting from the seeds sown in Eden. Physical pain and illness, emotional or psychological anguish, and spiritual crises also create genuine suffering in our lives, and should not be minimized.

Liz, for example, endures debilitating migraines and blindness as a result of a pear-sized tumor that killed her optic nerves. Chronic fatigue syndrome leaves Michael constantly exhausted, battling depression, and shelving his dreams because of a flat-lined energy level. David's diagnosis of bipolar depression followed months of manic spending and several suicide attempts, and wreaked havoc on his marriage, family, and finances. Ultimately he had to change jobs and move his family several hours away to start over.

Pain is real, and comparing pain is a dangerous and futile process. How tempting to look at another's suffering and say, "Yeah, I should have it so easy! You wouldn't believe what I'm going through." Or the reverse is possible, as well. Pain is pain, and it's interpreted by our spirit and body as pain regardless of the degree, severity, or type of suffering. To minimize the agony of a broken, or breaking, marriage because the neighbor's battle with cancer seems more serious puts the heartbroken in danger of a downward spiral. The husband whose wife left him for another man has valid pain; another's suffering should not diminish his trauma or force him into a place of denial.

To avoid a downward spiral or denial, we do well to recognize our bodies' attention-getting symptoms: taut nerves, tears, headaches, short tempers, out-of-proportion reactions, forgetfulness, fatigue, depression, inability to sleep, or sleeping too much. Richard Swenson writes in *Margin*, "Our pain is actually an ally of sorts. In the hurt is a help. Pain first gets our attention—as it does so well—and then moves us in the opposite direction of the danger."[3]

⊞ *Listen*

Therefore you, too, now have sorrow; but I will see you again, and your heart will rejoice, and no one takes your joy away from you. . . . These things I have spoken to you, that in Me you may have peace. In the world you have tribulation, but take courage; I have overcome the world.

John 16:22, 33

⊞ *Learn*

Man needs to suffer. When he does not have real griefs, he creates them. Griefs purify and prepare him.

José Martí, 1883

⊞ *Live*

✦ In what ways has suffering demanded your attention?

✦ What is your typical response to suffering or pain? To another's suffering or pain?

32. BETWEEN TWO GARDENS: PITFALLS OF PAIN

The question is, when suffering gets our attention, what do we do with it? Numerous pitfalls exist when we face off with our pain.

✦ *Idolize.* Donna created an idol of her pain. She was terrified to come close to the fire of her pain, but the flames crept ever closer. She feared that it would so destroy her life, burning her beyond recognition, that she could not live with the charred remains. She was afraid that, if she faced it, the suffering would consume her. If only she could dig trenches and saturate them with water and stand her ground, but pain so scarred her soul that she fabricated elaborate stories to push away reality. In this way, she circled her pain, bowing down to it, idolizing it.

✦ *Isolate.* Brendon's physical suffering was so intense that he pushed away the very people he loved the most, the people who could actually help him work through his crippling battle with arthritis. To isolate himself, he created conflict in his relationships and then nursed his hurt feelings, thus deflecting his attention from the real issue—his pain and decreasing mobility and his worth in God's sight.

✦ *Abandon Progress.* Another pitfall of suffering is that too much rummaging around in the basement of our pain could lead us to abandon the building process. When Israel was in exile, held captive in Babylon, King Cyrus issued a decree that the Israelites could return to Jerusalem to rebuild the temple. Nearly fifty thousand people responded and enthusiastically set about the restoration.

But the ruling government hired deconstruction specialists, who dug up the history of Israel and reported to the king that "if that city is rebuilt and the walls are finished, they will not pay tribute, custom, or toll, and it will damage the revenue of the kings" (Ezra 4:13). So the king issued a decree to halt the building, and "the people of the land discouraged the people of Judah, and frightened them from building" (Ezra 4:4). Progress was halted because the enemy excavated the past.

When we face our suffering and begin to rebuild our lives on this new foundation, others are forced to change the way they relate to us. Their perception and treatment of us inevitably changes, and possibly not for the better. Their reaction may be the equivalent of a wrecking ball to our spirit. Hopefully, though, our courageous response to suffering will encourage others to grow.

✦ *Messy*. Pain is rarely a clean-cut event, with a beginning, a middle, and an ending. Initially, it may even bring out the worst in us. Jan Dravecky, in writing about her own struggle with depression in the midst of her husband's battle with cancer, reassures us:

> Suffering is not tidy, because suffering is a purifying process, a process of cleansing out impurities. When suffering causes impurities to rise to the surface, naturally we are going to see the worst of people. Their selfishness is going to come out, their wrong priorities are going to become apparent, and they are not going to be able to mask their sinfulness anymore.[4]

✦ *Worthless Feelings*. Henri Nouwen reminds us that one of the blessings of pain is that in its midst we are wrapped in God's loving, affirming presence. We, unfortunately, are tempted to believe instead that brokenness points to our worthlessness:

> Once we are in touch with the blessing, we can live with our brokenness in a very different way. The great question of ministry and the spiritual life is to learn to live our brokenness under the blessing and not the curse. . . . Many live their brokenness under the curse. They don't think they are loved, or held safe, and so when suffering comes they see it as an affirmation of their worthlessness.[5]

Other pitfalls include the incredible slowness of the process of pain and the fact that suffering continues in one form or another. My friend Lynn says, "Our lives are like the Morton Salt commercial. When it rains, it pours." And finding the power of pain is largely a matter of perspective—it's called hindsight!

❈ *Listen*

But we have this treasure in earthen vessels, that the surpassing greatness of the power may be of God and not from ourselves; we are afflicted in every way, but not crushed; perplexed, but not despairing; persecuted, but not forsaken; struck down, but not destroyed; always carrying about in the body the dying of Jesus, that the life of Jesus also may be manifested in our body.

2 Corinthians 4:7–10

❈ *Learn*

I wanted to experience every kind of pain, bodily and spiritual, which I would have if I were to die—every fear and temptation. I intended this because I wanted to be purged by God's mercy and afterwards live more to his glory because of that sickness.

Julian of Norwich

❈ *Live*

✦ Which pitfalls of pain have you encountered? How do you avoid the pitfalls?

✦ How have you experienced God's presence in the midst?

33. POWER OF PAIN

A conversation with my then eight-year-old son highlighted for me the truth in the overused axiom, "No pain, no gain." Many nights Zak awakened us, moaning from the pain in his legs and shins. One morning I glanced up when he thundered down the stairs for school. I hugged him good morning, and said in surprise, "You've grown a foot!"

"Must be those growing pains," he said, standing up soldier straight. I laughed.

"Do you think they *were* growing pains, Mom?"

"Could be. I've heard they can be quite painful."

"I hope so," he stated.

"Why?"

"I don't want to go through all that pain for nothing. Might as well grow through it."

Whatever the type of pain, we can be bound by it or we can harness its power, allowing it to lead us into places we would never otherwise enter.

Pain has a focusing value, but its value depends on our point of focus. To concentrate on the agony is like looking in a "Magic Eye" poster for the hidden picture to appear, and seeing only the abstract, blurring particles. To see the hidden picture we have to focus on a point somewhere beyond the collage-like pieces.

Lamaze, a method of moving through labor and delivery natu-rally, carries the same principle. In Lamaze the woman gripped in birthing pain is trained to breathe evenly and to focus not on the pain but on a point beyond the pain, outside of herself, a place of beauty or interest.

With this in mind, then, Paul's words in 2 Corinthians 4:17–18 make sense: "For momentary, light affliction is producing for us an eternal weight of glory far beyond all comparison, while we look not at the things which are seen, but at the things which are not seen; for the things which are seen are temporal, but the things which are not seen are eternal."

Pain is a lesson in growth, in grace, and in trust. In suffering, we learn to focus on the *end* and not the means. Christ did not allow anguish to separate Him from God or to deflect His focus. To benefit from pain, we must allow pain to teach us about ourselves and about God. We can be tutored by adversity, as Lynn Austin shows in *My Father's God*. A wise rabbi responds to his anguished pupil's questions about suffering:

> You may certainly question Yahweh, but ask the right questions. . . . Ask Him what He wants to teach you through this suffering. Ask which of your faults, like pride or self-sufficiency or self-righteousness, He's trying to purge from you. Ask which of His eternal qualities, like love and compassion and forgiveness, He wants to burn into your heart. Yes, go ahead, ask questions! Ask why He gave you the talents and gifts that He did— your excellent mind, your ability to lead others. Ask Him what He wants you to do with your life.[6]

Perhaps we have been asking the wrong question. Rather than scrabbling around in the dirt and pebbles, asking "Will I be healed?" we need to dig more deeply, asking, "Will I be whole? Will I be holy?"

Ellis, an American soldier wounded in World War II, said, "Life is hard." His companion, Theo Lindheim, a German fighter pilot, said, "Yes. And that is the truth of it. You have lost your leg [for a better world] and the world is still a toilet. Your loss changes nothing, means nothing, unless it makes you a better man. This is why we suffer. Like a fire, it burns the filth of our souls away."[7]

We experience the power of pain when we learn to focus on God, grip tightly to His hand, and walk with Him through growth.

88 *Listen*

For He has not despised nor abhorred the affliction of the afflicted; neither has He hidden His face from him; but when he cried to Him for help, He heard.

Psalm 22:24

The Lord is near to the brokenhearted, and saves those who are crushed in spirit.

Psalm 34:18

88 *Learn*

I do not like this bitter path before me. Compliance to my own suffering galls me, but I know it is important for me to bow my head before this pain. . . . There is a work of God going on in me, and I must not use up the energies I need to hold myself constant to an attitude of surrender. I must use this little season of pain to learn how to identify with Christ's suffering. Yet admittedly, I slouch toward Jerusalem, I sleep in Gethsemane, I stand silent at Golgotha.

Karen Mains,
Comforting One Another in Life's Sorrows

✺ *Live*

◆ What has your pain or suffering taught you about yourself? About God?

◆ How have you chosen to focus?

◆ Where have you seen the power hidden beyond the pain?

34. FRUIT FROM SUFFERING

Though suffering is rooted in a life that is far below the life God imagined and designed us for, when we choose to let suffering fertilize and enrich our lives—choosing to "be holy, as He is holy"—our Gardener-Father brings forth fruit, not only in our lives, but in the lives of others. Seeing suffering as discipline allows us to wait more patiently for the fruit of discipline, a harvest of righteousness and peace (Hebrews 12:11).

Waiting, in the midst of discipline, forces us to rely on God. In Sunday school one day, Will said, "Desperation opens the door for faith in a way that nothing else does." Teresa nodded, adding, "My faith has been built by my suffering. We're more willing to hear what God has to say when we're in despair." This affirms Paul's words in 2 Corinthians 1:9 (NIV): "But this happened that we might not rely on ourselves but on God, who raises the dead." Augustine said, "In my deepest wound, I saw your glory and it dazzled me."

Joseph said when he named his son Ephraim, after triumphing in spite of being sold into slavery, "God has made me fruitful in the land of my affliction" (Genesis 41:52). This fruitfulness in our own lives extends, then, into the lives of others. "You intended to harm me," Joseph told his brothers later, "but God intended it for good to accomplish what is now being done, the saving of many lives" (50:20 NIV).

Suffering becomes significant when others' lives are impacted. A woman who was sexually abused as a teenager now has a ministry helping others with similar backgrounds. She has determined to share her secret shame that others might find healing.

> You have been damaged. But you have great hope. The mercy of God does not eradicate the damage, at least not in this life, but it soothes the soul and draws it forward to a hope that purifies and sets free. Allow the pain of the past and the travail of the change process to create fresh new life in you and to serve as a bridge over which another victim may walk from death to life.[8]

Suffering, in between the two gardens, becomes an opportunity to be transformed into the image of Christ, to rely on God and share His grace, and to intercede for others who are suffering or persecuted for His name's sake.

88 *Listen*

My son, do not make light of the Lord's discipline, and do not lose heart when he rebukes you, because the Lord disciplines those he loves. . . .

Endure hardship as discipline; God is treating you as sons. . . . God disciplines us for our good, that we may share in his holiness. No discipline seems pleasant at the time, but painful. Later on, however, it produces a harvest of righteousness and peace for those who have been trained by it.

Hebrews 12:5–7,10–11 NIV

⌗ *Learn*

In adversity our intellectual knowledge becomes actual knowledge. "Even though I walk . . . through the valley of the shadow of death, I will fear no evil, for you are with me. . . ." And now that you and I are walking through that valley we will learn if it is true. Adversity is the testing ground of our faith. God has to risk losing you forever to your anger and bitterness in order to have you for His true son. Anyone can believe and sing praises on the Temple mount when the sun is shining, but true praise is sung in the darkest valley when the Accuser tells you to curse God for making you suffer so much pain. If you can still praise your Father's goodness, even in the darkness, then you are His son indeed.

Lynn N. Austin,
My Father's God

⌗ *Live*

+ When have you experienced the significance of suffering?
+ How has it deepened you, making you more like Christ?
+ In what ways can your travail become a means of extending the love and grace of God to others?

35. THE END OF SUFFERING: CHRIST IN THE GARDEN OF GETHSEMANE

A lovely woman with huge waves of blond hair swept into the refreshment room at a recent retreat. She navigated over to the coffee cart, and we nodded, smiling, at one another. Within moments, her story spilled out. Her father died, she found her mother dead at the breakfast table three months later, and right after burying her mother, her husband had a heart attack. After being released to return to work, he had a second coronary and died. All within nine months. Issues with his children from a previous marriage compounded her grief and pain.

All this left her alone. Very alone.

When we moved into the room where the group worshiped, the only two chairs available were side by side. She followed me as we took our seats. As we sang and prayed, I glanced at my neighbor. Her head was bowed, tears streaming down her face. Almost highlighting her loneliness, her arms were wrapped around herself, clutching her rib cage, as if to hold herself together against the explosive grief.

I have many unanswered questions about suffering; looking back through my journals, I find example after example, life after life, where suffering seems endless and brutal and needless. And yet, though questions remain, we must somehow content ourselves to live in the unease of mystery, to live without all the answers.

Ultimately, we move closer to the Garden of Gethsemane when

we hold close the truth of Isaiah 53:5: "The punishment that brought us peace was upon him, and by his wounds we are healed" (NIV). We know that in some mysterious and inexplicable way, our sufferings are completed by Christ's work on the cross. First Peter 2:24 reminds us, "He himself bore our sins in His body on the cross, that we might die to sin and live to righteousness; for by his wounds you were healed."

One fact is irrefutable. Suffering is finite. One glorious day, we will live in a place where Christ's struggle in Gethsemane and hideous suffering in Jerusalem and on Golgotha, and his subsequent victory over darkness and evil, will catch up to our own lives. In heaven, we are promised, "He shall wipe away every tear from their eyes; and there shall no longer be any death; there shall no longer be any mourning, or crying, or pain; the first things have passed away" (Revelation 21:4).

88 *Listen*

So the ransomed of the Lord will return, and come with joyful shouting to Zion; and everlasting joy will be on their heads. They will obtain gladness and joy, and sorrow and sighing will flee away. I, even I, am He who comforts you.

Isaiah 51:11–12

O joy that seekest me through pain,
I cannot close my heart to thee;
I trace the rainbow through the rain,
and feel the promise is not vain
that morn shall tearless be.

George Matheson,
"O Love That Wilt Not Let Me Go"

❀ *Learn*

The disciple has no need to look for suffering; each disciple has a particular cross awaiting him. The sufferings of the Christian are defined by Christ—they involve, for example, bearing the sins of others in a ministry of forgiveness. It is not the suffering but the fellowship with Christ that is important; that is why the way of the disciples is seen as joyful and triumphant.

Haddon Willmer,
"Costly Discipleship,"
in *The Cambridge Companion to Dietrich Bonhoeffer*

❀ *Live*

✦ What questions do you have about suffering and Christ's fulfillment of suffering?

✦ When do you most doubt? When do you most trust?

✦ How do you sense God leading you to respond to suffering?

Ten

LIFE IN THE GARDEN

God's plan for life from the seeds of death sown in Eden never ends. He brings life to the tired and withered, hope to those without hope, meaning and purpose to those floundering. He finds us in our lostness, and guides us into a new, blooming place.

God's choices were always for life, forever; yet ours, because of those seeds, are naturally for death. Anytime we take life into our own hands we choose death, exile, separation from God. Look at Adam and Eve, who seized the fatal fruit hoping for godlike powers. If only they'd understood: they were made in the image of God! They didn't need to grasp and grapple with death. The waves of their death-choices spread from Eden through history, spilling into the very life of Christ in Gethsemane.

But God's plan, always for life, pounds triumphantly as we enter the Garden, where the new tomb is carved out of the rock. And so in our own lives, we find the miracle of miracles: Into this body of death, Christ has seeded His very own life, breathing into us the air of salvation and newness of spirit.

36. Eve in Eden

The hush of a new day rests over creation. In the predawn silence the first bird awakens, and a note, then two notes, break the stillness. A melody begins, a song of life and love to the Creator. The music crescendos and a man enters into the symphony, a being never before seen, envisioned only by the Three in Heaven. He goes about the work of examining each living creature, but shakes his head at every one. The Creator, the One who walks with him and whose eyes brighten with love at each interaction, reassures him. The man falls asleep, a deep sleep of peace and trust, and awakens to find beside him a woman.

Her first sensation is of warm breath, God breathing life into her nostrils. Her eyes flutter open, her heart beats with a sense of love for this Creator-God, who has poured life into her and through her.

They are man and woman. She has yet to be named, does not receive her name until they have roamed freely about the luscious Garden and sampled the fruit of the forbidden tree. Only after the results of their disobedience become clear in the form of the cursing of the ground and the promise that they will not live forever, but will taste death—only then is the woman given a name.

Adam calls her Eve. The "mother of all the living."

The woman, who tempted her husband and set death in motion, receives a name meaning "life" or "life producer." This is a stunning moment of fidelity for Adam—a declaration of forgiveness and faith.

Inherent in her name, Eve, is the promise that though her

choices resulted in death, spiritually and physically, for all of us, somehow, somewhere, down through the generations, life would return, the possibility of spiritual life. And though we each taste death as we return to the dust, we each, now, through the death and life of Christ Jesus, can experience life.

Even though we taste death, though we make choices daily that are death-choices: clinging to anger, or resentment, or lethargy; embracing selfishness, wrapping our arms around tangibles that money and work purchase; though we daily walk the line between life and death, we, too, whether man or woman, have the potential to be life producers.

Whether we ever reproduce physically, we have the choice to reap life, to sow seeds bearing fruit for eternity. By investing in the lives of others, seeing each encounter as a chance to give life, we, too, become life producers.

My friend Gail is a soul-model for me and a life producer. She demonstrates in every encounter the life and love she has received from a gracious and redeeming God. Recently we met for dinner, and her blue eyes sparkled with interest and humor. When the waiter came, she turned to him with animation and asked, "Is this a long-term career for you?" He responded instantly, opening the book of his life to her. He was a teacher, early elementary, this was a summer job, and he couldn't imagine doing anything other than teaching. When I commented to Gail later about her conversation starter, she said, "I try to develop a relationship with everyone I meet."

Her every interaction produces life.

Eve, though she set death in motion, was given the possibility of offering life. And we bear her trait—life giver—as we continue the legacy, as we find life in Christ and lead others to that life.

❈ *Listen*

But thanks be to God, who always leads us in triumphal procession in Christ and through us spreads everywhere the fragrance of the knowledge of him. For we are to God the aroma of Christ among those who are being saved and those who are perishing.

2 Corinthians 2:14–15 NIV

❈ *Look*

It is with each day of life that we chisel our influence into the hearts and lives of others. Christ is the artist. You are his tool. Only you can decide how you will allow the Master Craftsman to use your life. "One cannot transform a world except as individuals in the world are transformed, and individuals cannot be changed except as they are molded in the hands of the Master."

Pam Farrel,
Woman of Influence,
quoting Robert Coleman,
The Master Plan of Evangelism

❈ *Live*

◆ When do you choose death, rather than life?
◆ What happens within you when you hear yourself called life producer?
◆ When do you see God producing life, in you and through you in others?

37. FINDING LIFE BETWEEN
TWO GARDENS

In spite of the name life giver, death rippled quickly upon Eden's evacuation. Only when Eve's third child, Seth, had a son did people begin to once again call upon the name of the Lord. Like wayward dandelion fluff, the Israelites blew around on the winds of surrounding religions, practices, and morals (or lack thereof). Finally, after reaching the Promised Land for the second time and setting up the cities, their leader, Joshua, prepared to die. He called the people to take a stand: Would they serve the false gods of their imprisonment, the gods of the people beyond the river? Or would they serve the God who had delivered them from slavery into freedom, who provided shoes that never wore out and bread in the wilderness?

Joshua was stern with the Israelites and firm in his own choosing, and the Israelites responded with earnest humility.

So do we.

And then, like Joshua's fickle kinfolk, we forget to serve God, forget that each choice brings either life or death, and in the rocky, flowerless terrain between two gardens, we choose *self*. The old self, the selfish, self-focused "I love pity, I love to pout, I want to make you pay" self. A day of wallowing in this mud should convince us of life-choices. But we forget, again, when someone hurts or displeases or ignores us. And we choose to serve ourselves, not God.

So it goes. A rigorous, exhausting, self-defeating circling of good intentions vying with egocentric hearts, like boxers in a ring.

Choosing life also means choosing death, a paradox; choosing to die to temporary pleasures, to self-indulgence at another's expense. But this is true in the garden, every garden: "What you sow does not come to life unless it dies. When you sow, you do not plant the body that will be, but just a seed, perhaps of wheat or of something else" (1 Corinthians 15:36–37 NIV). We don't sow oak trees, we drop acorns into the ground. The acorn itself dies and then becomes a new form of life, a tree.

I hate this truth. But it is so: We must die to ourselves in order to live a new life in Christ Jesus. And daily, we must choose life. Thankfully, though we take the fruit into our own hands, demanding our own way, we can also daily choose to move back into the presence of Christ, the One who died, that we might ever live.

88 *Listen*

" 'And I gave you a land on which you had not labored, and cities which you had not built, and you have lived in them; you are eating of vineyards and olive groves which you did not plant.'

"[Joshua said,] 'Now, therefore, fear the Lord and serve Him in sincerity and truth; and put away the gods which your fathers served beyond the River and in Egypt, and serve the Lord. And if it is disagreeable in your sight to serve the Lord, choose for yourselves today whom you will serve . . . as for me and my house, we will serve the Lord.' "

Joshua 24:13–15

🞲 *Learn*

LIFE-CHOICES

Choose You This Day:
Encouragement not criticism
A smile not a frown
Forgiveness not resentment
Love not hatred
Praise not pouting
Relationship not isolation
Letting go not clinging
Grace not grousing
Growth not stasis
Dances not dirges
Feasts of spirit not famine
Beauty not ugliness
Servanthood not self-focus

Jane Rubietta

🞲 *Live*

+ When is it most difficult to choose life? Is there one area, one relationship, of primary struggle?
+ When have you experienced life-giving choices and the empowerment of Christ?

38. CHRIST IN THE GARDEN

In the Garden of Eden, Adam chose to disobey, setting death in motion. When Jesus chose obedience, He reversed the whole process. Christ's death set *life* in motion. His entire purpose was redemption: to fulfill that which began in Eden, to bring to an end the curses resulting from Adam and Eve's capitulation. His whole life propelled Him to the work done in Gethsemane, then to the hill shaped like a skull, and on into the Garden in which was a new tomb. A now-empty tomb.

From the time when Christ breathed His last breath, and the earth quaked and the veil split in half from top to bottom and the earth gave up its dead—from that time until we return to the tomb on Sunday, the first day of the week, indeed, the first day of new life, we have no record. The court reporters and the paparazzi and the photojournalists were barred entrance from the final round, when Christ wrestled with the Serpent; when He fulfilled the promise in Genesis 3:15: "He shall bruise you on the head, and you shall bruise him on the heel."

Here's what we do know, however: That with His momentous appearance from the dead, Christ fulfilled the Law, abolished the curse, and stands, the risen Lord, having canceled the death sentence, crushed the Serpent, and become our light and our bread and our rest. He has despised the shame of the cross and given us tools to stand against the disfigurement of shame. Jesus established for us the possibility of walking in unbroken fellowship with God. The Light of the World has withstood the darkness of temptation, treason, violence, and night. Jesus lived the life of an exile, died the death of a criminal and a scapegoat, being crucified outside the gates. His entire life and even His death looked like a failure, yet it was in truth a resolution of all the curses and problems that had sprouted up since Eden.

And here's something else, one more amazing fulfillment, one more evidence of God's provision for us from Eden to Gethsemane. When God created Adam and Eve, He breathed the breath of life into them. Outside of Eden, en route to the Promised Land, the breath of God dried up the Red Sea so the Israelites could cross on dry ground. And when Jesus hung there, on the cross, He "uttered a loud cry, and breathed His last. . . . And when the centurion, who was standing right in front of Him, saw the way He breathed His last, he said, 'Truly this man was the Son of God.' " (Mark 15:37, 39). His very breath bore witness to His identity.

But the story doesn't stop there. When Christ appeared to the disciples after triumphing over the grave, He found them cowering in a closed room for "fear of the Jews." Twice He told them, "Peace be with you" (John 20:19–21). And then, "As the Father has sent Me, I also send you." And when He had said this, *He breathed on them*, and said to them, "Receive the Holy Spirit." With that breath, Christ reestablished the permanent presence of God within the believer, enabling each of us to live fully in the Garden of Life.

Christ's work in the Garden, His very breath, is an invitation to us: to move out of the Garden where life became death and into the Garden where death became life.

🖇 *Listen*

We were therefore buried with him through baptism into death in order that, just as Christ was raised from the dead through the glory of the Father, we too may live a new life.

Romans 6:4 NIV

88 *Learn*

So the cross not only brings Christ's life to an end, it ends also the first life, the old life, of every one of His true followers. It destroys the old pattern, the Adam pattern, in the believer's life, and brings it to an end. Then the God who raised Christ from the dead raises the believer and a new life begins.

A. W. Tozer,
The Root of Righteousness

88 *Live*

- ✦ Where do you need the life-giving breath of Christ right now?
- ✦ How are you traversing the land between Eden and Gethsemane?
- ✦ What do you see God doing during the journey?

39. FUTURE IN THE GARDEN

Crushing fatigue bowed my body as I sat one day during a layover in Birmingham's airport. Like a horse sleeps standing up, my head bobbed over my work. I tried to write in my journal, but my eyelids closed like trapdoors whose springs were broken. I refocused, then opened the Scriptures to Matthew 28:1–10, which tells the story of Mary Magdalene and another Mary. As sunrise shattered the dark of night, the two Marys made their way to the garden tomb. They knew its location, because they sat watch over the tomb when Jesus was buried. They also knew a huge stone sealed the entrance.

But an angel of the Lord had rolled away the stone and now perched atop it. The guards shook with fear and became like dead men, the Scriptures say, because the angel's appearance was like lightning, and his garment as white as snow. And to the women, the angel's first words were, "Do not be afraid." (He did not so reassure the quaking guards!) The angel then delivered the Lord's message to the women: "He is not here, for He has risen, just as He said. Come, see the place where He was lying. And go quickly and tell His disciples that He has risen from the dead; and behold, He is going before you into Galilee, there you will see Him; behold, I have told you."

The two Marys ran "with fear and great joy" into the future, into their calling. I tensed with the conflicting emotions, felt the pulling on the heart, the rapid beating of the pulse. Not much is known about the other Mary, but for Mary Magdalene, life had meant death until meeting Jesus; now His death threatened to undo everything. She lost her future, standing at the cross, watching at the tomb. She thought her life over, her future dead, with her Lord crucified and buried. But as she ran in obedience into her calling as the first evangelist, the bearer of good news—He is risen, just as He said!—she ran straight into Jesus himself. And His words?

"Do not be afraid."

While we, too, lost our future in Eden, in the Garden after Gethsemane we hear the first calling: "Go and tell the others" (see

John 19:41, 20:17). What is our response, in light of our journey through the gardens of God?

Whatever the future holds, the Lord Jesus himself goes before us into it, even as He went before Mary. And if Christ is with us in the future, then truly we can heed the angel's words, and the very words of Christ: "Do not be afraid." And we can run with joy, even in the midst of fear.

The Joy Watch

There in the airport, a major project was wrapping up. My future was uncertain; this project had been life-giving, and financially supporting, for nearly a year. Especially in weariness, despair leans close, and I confess to both a fear of that future and a dimming of joy.

Suddenly, a child's squeal jerked my heart to life. Every child's squeal becomes my own child's, and I leaned around a pillar to see. A little boy—possibly two years old, with a shock of thick, black hair and lovely olive skin—moved away from his mother, hands outstretched and reaching, eyes alight. His smile beamed joy through my system. He headed for something beyond my sight. The mother hesitated, started to pull him onto the moving walkway with her, trying to stay on task. Then she nodded, receiving some unseen assurance from behind the pole, and let him toddle ahead with glee.

I leaned further around the column to put a complete visual with the audible joy. The toddler stood eye to eye with a calm, puppy-sized lab on a leash. The puppy put a wet muzzle to the entranced boy's nose, and tiny hands stroked the chocolate, velvet ears. They stood this way, puppy and boy, loving each other, fast friends.

I thought I would pop with joy. My face stretched tight with an enormous smile, and I glanced about to appreciate the moment with other observers.

Cell phones and laptops and file folders occupied the heads all around. They'd missed a moment in a million. So, nearly, had I, washed with fatigue as I was.

I kept watch, then, and try to do so now, when fear of the future or preoccupation drain me. A joy watch. Keeping watch that day, tears nearly spurted when I saw the girl with the bulging backpack talking with animation to the parents flanking her sides.

A dad carrying a baby. More joy pounded.

A tall father exclaimed, picked up a preteen girl off the people-mover, kissed her loudly, and pressed her to his chest. They strode off together, he altering his steps and his posture to bend near, to catch every nuance.

I felt as if the Holy Spirit came upon me, flooding me with a joy that had been dormant, like a tree in winter suddenly greeting the sun with billions of blossoms.

The last joy watch that day, before I boarded the plane: happy, high-pitched, girlish screaming turned my head. Two flight attendants hurled themselves into each other's arms and laughed and cried to see each other. What a beautiful scene of friendship—exuberant, loud, unashamed, flushed of face, and smiling nonstop.

Perhaps, I thought, that was how Mary wanted to greet her Lord and Teacher.

✾ *Listen*

I have set the Lord continually before me;
Because He is at my right hand, I will not be shaken.
Therefore my heart is glad, and my glory rejoices;

My flesh also will dwell securely.
For Thou wilt not abandon my soul to Sheol;
Neither wilt Thou allow Thy Holy One to see the pit.
Thou wilt make known to me the path of life;
In Thy presence is fulness of joy;
In Thy right hand there are pleasures forever.

Psalm 16:8–11

Now, all these things are from God, who reconciled us to Himself through Christ, and gave us the ministry of reconciliation, namely, that God was in Christ reconciling the world to Himself, not counting their trespasses against them, and He has committed to us the word of reconciliation. Therefore, we are ambassadors for Christ, as though God were entreating through us; we beg you on behalf of Christ, be reconciled to God. He made Him who knew no sin to be sin on our behalf, that we might become the righteousness of God in Him.

2 Corinthians 5:18–21

88 *Learn*

Passion is the roller coaster ride that can happen when you follow Jesus Christ. It is the breathtaking, thrill-filled, bone-rattling ride of a lifetime where every moment matters and all you can do is hang on for dear life. When you become a Christian, when you decide to follow Christ, you decide in favor of passion. Jesus came to forgive us of our sin, yes, but His mission was also to introduce us to the passion of living. Most people believe that following Jesus is all about living right. Not true. *Following Jesus is all about living* fully.

Michael Yaconelli,
Dangerous Wonder

⊠ *Live*

♦ What fears of the future pound in your heart?

♦ Where is Jesus in the midst of your fear, and what does He say to you?

♦ What calling do you sense as fear mingles with joy?

40. A LIVING HOPE

In this Garden, in the Garden where there is a new tomb, in the Garden where Christ has been raised from the dead, no cherubim with flaming sword waits to bar entrance, as in Eden. In this Garden, the angel meets us and says to us, "Do not be afraid" (Matthew 28:5). After the Resurrection, every instance of Jesus' interactions with others was full of grace and peace. He said repeatedly, "Do not fear," and "Peace be with you" (see John 20:19, 21, 26; Matthew 28:10). The triumphant Christ demonstrates resurrection life: If He has conquered the last enemy, death, we truly have nothing to fear.

Restoration

In Eden, God created Adam and Eve joyfully, generously, in His image. After their sin, Adam and Eve's children were born in their own image. How this broke God's heart. And yet, the Garden—of Eden, and of Gethsemane—is about life, about newness of life. Throughout the Scriptures, we hear God promising, "Behold, I will do something new, now it will spring forth; will you not be aware of it? I will even make a roadway in the wilderness, rivers in the desert"

(Isaiah 43:19). We find Christ assuring us, "I am the resurrection and the life; he who believes in Me shall live even if he dies" (John 11:25). "I will give you a new heart and put a new spirit within you" (Ezekiel 36:26). "Old things passed away; behold, new things have come" (2 Corinthians 5:17).

God does not sow death in this Garden—except the death of that defaced image. In Christ, also called "the last Adam," the very image of God, we find that we are made new, that all our lives are about being transformed into the image of Christ. "For as in Adam all die, so also in Christ all shall be made alive" (1 Corinthians 15:22).

The image, rubbed out in Eden, is being restored daily as we move closer to the completion of Christ's work in Gethsemane. After traveling from Eden to Gethsemane, the truth breaks open tomb-cold hearts: The entire journey between these two gardens is about restoration; restoring us to the image of God, that we might again walk with Him in newness of life. And we know, now, that everything we encounter en route to the Garden—every rock, thistle, snake—is a gardening tool to continue bringing forth in us the image of Christ.

What can we say to this? "Blessed be the God and Father of our Lord Jesus Christ, who according to His great mercy has caused us to be born again to a living hope through the resurrection of Jesus Christ from the dead" (1 Peter 1:3).

My friend, I invite you: Come to the Garden, and walk with Jesus in newness of life. And in the final Garden, I will be there, too, and we will walk together, and we will never tire of telling the story of Christ's life, in us, with us, and for us, in the Garden.

⌘ *Listen*

The Lord will comfort Zion; He will comfort all her waste places. And her wilderness He will make like Eden, and her desert like the garden of the Lord. Joy and gladness will be found in her, thanksgiving and sound of a melody.

Isaiah 51:3

Death cannot keep its prey,
Jesus my Savior,
He tore the bars away,
Jesus my Lord!
Up from the grave He arose
With a mighty triumph o'er His foes
He arose a victor from the dark domain
And He lives forever with His saints to reign.
He arose! He arose!
Hallelujah! Christ arose!

Robert Lowry,
"Up from the Grave He Arose"

⌘ *Learn*

[Two little people with deformed bodies who live with much physical pain are yet devout Christians, and one of them prays the following prayer:]

O Father of life, we praise Thee that one day Thou will take Thy poor crooked creatures, and give them bodies like Christ's, perfect as His, and full of Thy light. Help us to grow faster—as fast as Thou canst help us grow. Help us to keep our eyes on the opening of Thy hand, that we may know the manna when it comes. O Lord, we rejoice that we are Thy

making, though Thy handiwork is not very clear in the outer man as yet.
We bless Thee that we feel Thy hand making us. What if it be in pain!
Evermore we hear the voice of the Potter above the human grind of His
wheel. Father, Thou only knowest how we love Thee. Fashion the clay to
Thy beautiful will. To the eyes of men we are vessels of dishonor, but we
know Thou dost not despise us. Thou has made us love Thee, and hope in
Thee, and in Thy love we will be brave and endure. All in good time, O
Lord. Amen.

George MacDonald,
Paul Faber, Surgeon

❖ *Live*

+ Where do you need a sense of Christ's peaceful presence now?
+ Describe yourself, made new in the image of Christ.
+ If you could sum up your journey in a paragraph, how would it read? Is there someone with whom you could share that journey?

ENDNOTES

Chapter One: Creation in the Garden

1. Edward M. Hallowell, M.D., *Connect: 12 Vital Ties That Open Your Heart, Lengthen Your Life, and Deepen Your Soul.* (New York: Pantheon Books, 1999), 222.

2. Warren Wiersbe, *With the Word: A Devotional Commentary* (Nashville: Thomas Nelson, 1991), 19.

3. George MacDonald, *Unspoken Sermons (Series Three)*, (London: Longmans, Green, and Co., 1895), 221.

4. G. K. Chesterton, *Tremendous Trifles*, as quoted in George Marlin, Richard Rabatin, and John Swan, eds., *The Quotable Chesterton* (San Francisco: Ignatius Press, 1986), 197.

5. G. K. Chesterton, *Chaucer* (Kansas City, Mo.: Sheed and Ward, 1956) as quoted in *The Quotable Chesterton*, 115.

6. Bob Condor, "Feeling Better Might Mean Seeing the Light," *Chicago Tribune*, June 25, 2000, Section 13, 3.

7. Patch Adams, M.D., with Maureen Mylander, *Gesundheit!*

(Rochester, Vt.: Healing Arts Press, 1998), 45.

8. Mary S. Edgar, "God Who Touchest Earth with Beauty," *United Methodist Hymnal*, 1964.

Chapter Three: Darkness in the Garden

1. Amy Tan, *The Joy Luck Club* (New York: Putnam, 1989), 67, 83.
2. As quoted in *Contemplating the Cross*, by Tricia McCary Rhodes (Minneapolis: Bethany House Publishers, 1998), 61.

Chapter Four: Shame in the Garden

1. Ronald Potter-Efron and Patricia Potter-Efron, *Letting Go of Shame* (New York: HarperCollins, 1989), 1.
2. *Ryrie Study Bible*, footnote on Deuteronomy 21:23.

Chapter Five: Sacrifice in the Garden

1. For more on the sacrificial system, read Leviticus 1–6, and read about the feasts in Leviticus 23.
2. Archbishop Fulton J. Sheen, *The Eternal Galilean*. As quoted in *The Journey Toward God*, ed. Benedict J. Groeschel, CFR, with Kevin Perrotta (Ann Arbor, Mich.: Servant Publications, 2000), 80.

Chapter Seven: Failure in the Garden

1. Father John Powell, *Happiness Is an Inside Job* (Allen, Tex.: Tabor Publishing, 1989), 25.

Chapter Eight: Exile and the Garden

1. John W. deGruchy, ed. *The Cambridge Companion to Dietrich Bonhoeffer*. "The Life of Dietrich Bonhoeffer," by F. Burton Nelson (Cambridge, UK: Cambridge University Press, 1999), 43.
2. Ibid., 261.
3. Lynn N. Austin, *Among the Gods* (Kansas City, Mo.: Beacon Hill Press, 1998), 273–279.

Chapter Nine: Suffering in the Garden

1. As quoted by Tim Woodruff in *Walk This Way* (Colorado Springs: NavPress, 1999), 177.
2. Get a copy of *Please Pray for Us*, by Johan Companjen (Minneapolis: Bethany House Publishers, 2000). It is a tremendous almanac of the world's most persecuted countries, complete with statistics, stories, and specific prayer requests.
3. Richard Swenson, *Margin: Restoring Emotional, Physical, Financial, and Time Reserves to Overloaded Lives* (Colorado Springs: NavPress, 1992), 17.
4. Jan Dravecky, *A Joy I'd Never Known* (Grand Rapids, Mich.: Zondervan Publishing House, 1996), 177.
5. Stephen Kendrick, "In Touch With the Blessing: An Interview With Henri Nouwen," *The Christian Century* (Mar. 24–31, 1993, Vol. 10), 10.
6. Lynn N. Austin, *My Father's God* (Kansas City, Mo.: Beacon Hill Press, 1997), 179–180.

7. Bodie Thoene, *In My Father's House* (Minneapolis: Bethany House Publishers, 1992), 112.

8. Dan Allender, *The Wounded Heart: Hope for Adult Victims of Childhood Sexual Abuse* (Colorado Springs: NavPress, 1990), 247.

WORKS CITED

The publisher gratefully acknowledges permission to reproduce material from the following sources. While every effort has been made to secure permissions, we may have failed in a few cases to trace or contact the copyright holder. We apologize for any inadvertent oversight or error.

Dan Allender. *The Wounded Heart: Hope for Adult Victims of Childhood Sexual Abuse*. Colorado Springs, CO: NavPress, 1990.

Ray S. Anderson. *The Gospel According to Judas: Is There a Limit to God's Forgiveness?* Colorado Springs, CO: NavPress, 1991.

Brother Andrew. *For the Love of my Brothers*. Minneapolis, MN: Bethany House Publishers, 1998.

Lynn N. Austin. *My Father's God*. Kansas City, MO: Beacon Hill Press, 1997.

G. K. Chesterton. *Chaucer*. Kansas City, MO: Sheed & Ward, 1956.

———. *Lunacy and Letters*. Kansas City, MO: Sheed & Ward, 1958.

———. *Tremendous Trifles*. Chester Springs, PA: Dufour Editions, 1968.

Jan Dravecky. *A Joy I'd Never Known*. Grand Rapids, MI: Zondervan Publishing House, 1996.

Ronald Potter-Efron and Patricia Potter-Efron. *Letting Go of Shame*. New York: HarperCollins, 1989.

John W. deGruchy, ed. *The Cambridge Companion to Dietrich Bonhoeffer*. "The Life of Dietrich Bonhoeffer," by F. Burton Nelson. Cambridge, UK: Cambridge University Press, 1999. "Prayer and Action for Justice: Bonhoeffer's Spirituality" by Geffrey B. Kelly.

Pam Farrel. *Woman of Influence: Ten Traits of Those Who Want to Make a Difference*. Downers Grove, IL: InterVarsity Press, 1996.

Edward M. Hallowell, M.D. *Connect: 12 Vital Ties That Open Your Heart, Lengthen Your Life, and Deepen Your Soul*. New York: Pantheon Books, 1999.

Robert Hemfelt, Ed.D., Frank Minerth, M.D., and Paul Meier, M.D. *We Are Driven: The Compulsive Behaviors America Applauds*. Nashville: Thomas Nelson, 1991.

Stephen Kendrick. "In Touch With the Blessing: An Interview With Henri Nouwen," *The Christian Century* (Mar. 24–31, 1993, vol. 11, o. 10).

Karen Mains. *Comforting One Another in Life's Sorrows*. Nashville: Thomas Nelson, 1997.

George Marlin, Richard Rabatin, John Swan, eds. *The Quotable Chesterton: A Topical Compilation of the Wit, Wisdom, and Satire of G. K. Chesterton*. San Francisco: Ignatius Press, 1986.

Tricia McCary Rhodes. *Contemplating the Cross: A Pilgrimage of Prayer*. Minneapolis, MN: Bethany House Publishers, 1998.

———. *Taking Up Your Cross: The Incredible Gain of the Crucified Life*. Minneapolis, MN: Bethany House Publishers, 2000.

Alexander Schmemann. *For the Life of the World*. Crestwood, NY: St.

Vladimir Seminary Press, 1973.

Archbishop Fulton J. Sheen. *The Eternal Galilean*. Staten Island, NY: The Alba House, 1934.

Richard Swenson. *Margin: Restoring Emotional, Physical, Financial, and Time Reserves to Overloaded Lives*. Colorado Springs, CO: NavPress, 1992.

Amy Tan. *The Joy Luck Club*. New York: Putnam Publishing Group, 1989.

Bodie Thoene. *In My Father's House*. Minneapolis, MN: Bethany House Publishers, 1992.

A. W. Tozer. *The Pursuit of God*. Harrisburg, PA: Christian Publications, Inc, n.d.

———. *The Root of Righteousness*. Harrisburg, PA: Christian Publications, Inc., 1955.

Joseph L. Umidi. *Confirming the Pastoral Call*. Grand Rapids, MI: Kregel Publications, 2000.

Douglas D. Webster. *SoulCraft: How God Shapes Us Through Relationships*. Downers Grove, IL: InterVarsity Press, 1999.

Warren Wiersbe. *With the Word: A Devotional Commentary*. Nashville: Thomas Nelson, 1991.

Michael Yaconelli. *Dangerous Wonder: The Adventure of Childlike Faith*. Colorado Springs, CO: NavPress, 1998.

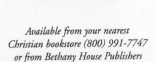
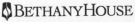